THE SECRET OF THEATRICAL SPACE

Orff. Prometheus. *Staatsoper, Munich, 1968. Dir: August Everding.*

THE SECRET OF THEATRICAL SPACE

The Memoirs of
Josef Svoboda

Edited and translated

by

J. M. Burian

An Applause Original

THE SECRET OF THEATRICAL SPACE

Copyright © 1993 by Josef Svoboda

I should like to acknowledge the significant work of Dr. Milena Honzíková, Svoboda's literary collaborator, in sorting out and organizing Svoboda's varied notes, sustained writing, and previously published material that constituted the raw material of the Czech text. I also thank her for helpful elucidation of certain passages in the text. Similar thanks are due my colleague, Professor Mojmir Frinta. I gratefully acknowledge the support provided to my research and travel related to this project by the University at Albany of the State University of New York. The editorial assistance of Applause Books in sharpening many details has been most welcome, particularly the suggestions of Glenn Young and Greg Collins. And I wish to express my deep thanks to Grayce Susan Burian for her unstinting assistance in transcribing and editing this text.

—Jarka M. Burian

Library of Congress Cataloging-in-Publication Data

Svoboda, Josef, 1920-
    [Tajemství divadelního prostoru. English]
    The secret of theatrical space / Josef Svoboda ; translated and
edited by J.M. Burian.
      p.   cm.
    "An Applause original."
    Includes bibliographical references (p.) and index.
    ISBN 1-55783-137-8 : $45.00
    1. Svoboda, Josef 1920- . 2. Theaters--Stage--setting and
scenery. 3. Set designers--Czechoslovakia. I. Burian, Jarka,
1927- . II. Title.
PN2096.S9A3   1992
792' .025'092--dc20   92-27220
                                             CIP

British Library Cataloguing-in Publication Data

A catalogue record for this book is available from the British Library.

APPLAUSE THEATRE BOOK PUBLISHERS

211 W. 71st Street
New York, NY 10023
Phone: (212) 595-4735   Fax: (212) 721-2856

406 Vale Road
Tonbridge KENT TN9 1XR
Phone: 0732 357755   Fax: 0732 770219

FIRST APPLAUSE PRINTING: 1993

CONTENTS

PREFACE

Svoboda is first and foremost a creative artist still actively engaged in his career, working at home and abroad on six to twelve stage productions annually. Now in his seventies, he also remains artistic head of Laterna Magika, a production organization devoted to the creative interplay of live and filmed action—the "dialogue between projection screen and actor," as he has put it. (Svoboda also was, from 1969 until 1990, a professor of architecture in Prague's School of Applied and Industrial Arts.)

The Secret of Theatrical Space is less a methodical exposition of his career and the theoretical implications of his work than a narrative memoir of Svoboda's experiences in twentieth-century theatre, enriched by his observations on the principal concepts and techniques that have characterized his work. Throughout, Svoboda shares with us his memories, spectrum of experiences, satisfactions and disappointments, as with an interested, friendly acquaintance. He lets us in on the partly scientific, partly inspirational, phases of the collective art of theatre production that culminate, when all conditions are right, in the *magic* he sees as essential to all art, but above all, to theatre.

After providing a panoramic view of the chief milestones of his career, Svoboda settles down in his culminating chapter, "Scenography," to explore more thoroughly and deeply the poetics of his scenographic art and to confide in us some of his most provocative insights and convictions. Because this chapter is so charged with Svoboda's essential theories and principles, it was decided to place it "up front" in this edition, before his review of his evolution as an artist and his account of his chief collaborative efforts.

Svoboda's writing style ranges from scientific precision to near poetic stream of consciousness: a mixture of reminiscence, objective description, analytical explanation, and intuitive vision. His customary exactness occasionally gives way to metaphoric, elliptical, and even elusive expression. As if he were talking informally to the reader, he is likely to initiate a theme or account, drop it in order to develop a related matter or two, and then return to the initial point. This discursive mode is a reflection of the man himself. He places enormous emphasis on the need of a disciplined, methodical, logical foundation for true creativity; yet he insists on the crucial role of intuition and last-minute inspiration. Although he consistently applies scientific principles and high-tech innovation to his work, Svoboda also remains something of a mystic in his sensitivity to the latent forces within the interplay of space, time, movement, and light on stage—as the very title of this book suggests.

Virtually all of Svoboda's writing for this book occurred by early 1988, well before the Velvet Revolution of late 1989 with its overthrow of the Communist regime that had ruled Czechoslovakia since 1948. This accounts for an occasional guardedness or indirectness when he touches on the socio-political climate of various eras or refers to less than ideal working conditions or morale in Czech theatre, especially in the past two decades. In his work and in his writing Svoboda consistently strove to remain apolitical, insofar as that disposition was possible. But it is worth noting that in the hectic early hours of the Velvet Revolution, Svoboda put the quarters and facilities of his Laterna Magika theatre at the disposal of Václav Havel and the Civic Forum movement. Typically, it was done without fanfare.

In many respects, the Communist regime was generous to the arts, but almost always at a heavy price. Although he could easily have secured lucrative, permanent employment beyond the iron curtain, Svoboda chose to retain his base of operations and his home in Prague, and to resist the status quo from within rather than without as an overt dissenter. Not the least of his reasons for staying was his intense identification with his native culture—his "cradle," as he has put it. Svoboda's feeling for his roots—personal and professional—is particularly apparent as he describes his

Svoboda in the late 1970s.

early years and experiences. His love of nature, his respect for craftsmanship and order, his feeling for raw materials, like wood, that serve theatre, and his acute responsiveness to the properties of space and light were all part of his boyhood in Čáslav. "I perceived light physically, not only visually," Svoboda has said. "For me, light became a substance."

Equally significant in Svoboda's evolution as a theatre artist were the scenographic traditions he inherited. Without consciously doing so, he followed along paths pioneered by Appia, Craig, and the artists of the Bauhaus and early Soviet theatre. More immediately, in Czechoslovakia itself, Svoboda could draw on a rich, architecturally grounded stage design practice. Influenced by avant-garde staging in both western European and Soviet theatres of the '20s and early '30s, the Czech theatre consistently incorporated expressive stage settings as an integral component of production. Indeed, it took the lead in this regard during the 1930s as repressive political forces gained strength elsewhere in Europe. Svoboda indicates his admiration for several important earlier Czech designers in this book (e.g., Vlastislav Hofman, František Tröster); others he has admired include Antonin Heythum, Bedřich Feuerstein, František Muzika, and František Zelenka. All but Muzika were trained as architects.

The term "scenography" is a loaded one for Svoboda. Inherent within it are a group of premises and values that form the core of Svoboda's artistic credo. His usage of it in this book is rather flexible, ranging from reference to a

disciplines, such as painting, sculpture, graphic art, or, above all, architecture, for the scenographer's primary challenge is that of defining, controlling, and transforming space.

The scenographer, moreover, should also be able to think as a director; he must be concerned with the ways in which his scenic proposals will *function dramatically* in the evolving stage action. Scenography is not concerned with scenery as mere decor or as a static illustration of place. A stage setting should be a dynamic, transformable component of the total dramatic action, very much an "actor" in the performance.

The scenographer must also be conversant with a broad range of today's technological materials, instruments, and techniques so as to make scenography as expressive and responsive as possible to the demands of the text and the director, the ultimate sources of authority in any production.

Svoboda himself would add a few other characteristics to an ideal portrait of a scenographer: humility, a dedication to experimentation, and a commitment to conveying a sense of

Shakespeare. As You Like It. *National Theatre, Prague, 1970. Dir: Jaromir Pleskot. The background was formed by various projections onto layers of wire netting.*

complex concept to a virtual synonym for stage design, scenery, or setting. In its historic sense, scenography for Svoboda relates back to the Renaissance and Baroque masters, such as Serlio, Sabbatini, Torelli, and the Bibienas, men who were architects and engineers, who brought scientific method and technological expertise to the service of scenic art. Conceptually, a scenographer is not merely a visual artist interested in theatre, but one who has mastered the principles of design in relation to one of the "harder"

the present. The ultimate goal of scenography is not a razzle-dazzle tour de force of spectacle that shows off the talents of the scenographer in his quest for personal expression. Scenography is like a musical instrument put at the disposal of the orchestra of the production, an instrument which has been shaped during a long, intense study of the script in consultation with the director, and which is likely to evolve further during the rehearsal process. Each production, therefore, even a broad farce, is

Prokofiev. Romeo and Juliet *(ballet). National Theatre, Prague, 1971. Chor: P. Weigl. Still another variation of a suspended cyclorama, but here a practicable construction used by the performers.*

seemed the most important names and terms mentioned by Svoboda. In doing so, I have limited myself to the names of *some* of the many Czechs who shared in Svoboda's rich career, for it would not have been feasible to provide data on all to whom he refers. I have not provided information in the Glossary on any of Svoboda's non-Czech collaborators, partly because they are probably familiar to English speaking readers and partly because Svoboda usually provides sufficient information himself.

I have also added a chronological list of essential data on all of Svoboda's productions, starting with his earliest work in Prague. Any such list can be only approximately definitive in view of partial records, postponed openings, and occasionally inadequate distinction between a first public performance (e.g., a preview) and an official premiere. When a production seems to appear more than once, it is assumed that the later productions have varied from the original in several respects.

Further information and comment in English relating to most of the productions mentioned by Svoboda may be found in one or more of my previous studies focusing on him: *The Scenography of Josef Svoboda* (Wesleyan UP,

to be approached as a serious challenge—and, always, as an experiment, rather than as a routine variation on tried and true methods. And whatever the historical setting of the work by the playwright, the scenography ought to convey a sense of "today," whether in its materials, its application of contemporary techniques, or its style.

This composite ideal is not always readily attained, even by Svoboda. The elemental, intuitive state that underlies even his most complex, calculated efforts was perhaps best expressed in a recent European television feature devoted to Svoboda. Its final moments show him sitting in the empty orchestra of the Smetana Theatre, where he began his professional career in 1945. As the lights gradually darken, we hear his thoughts via a voice-over:

> When I sit alone in a theatre and gaze into the dark space of its empty stage, I'm frequently seized by fear that this time I won't manage to penetrate it. And I always hope that this fear will never desert me. Without an unending search for the key to the secret of creativity, there is no creation. It's necessary always to begin again. And that is beautiful.

In translating Svoboda's manuscript from its Czech galleys, I have made a few cuts and transpositions in the text to achieve greater clarity. For the same reason, I have also included occasional footnotes to update or amplify certain references; and I have added a Glossary of what

Dürrenmatt. The Anabaptists. *National Theatre, Prague, 1968. Dir: Miroslav Macháček. The wooden ribs of the globe captured the world of the sixteenth-century sect.*

Beckett. Waiting for Godot. *Salsberg Festspiele, 1970. Dir: Otomar Krejča. The architecture of the auditorum was continued onto the stage, much as it was in the scenography for the Prague, 1969 Don Giovanni. Here, a mirror formed the backdrop.*

1971); *Svoboda:Wagner* (Wesleyan UP, 1983); and in the following journals:

"Josef Svoboda: Theatre Artist in an Age of Science." *Educational Theatre Journal* 22.2 (May 1970): 123-145.

"A Scenographer's Work: Josef Svoboda's Designs, 1971-1975." *Theatre Design and Technology* 12.2 (Summer 1976): 11-34.

"Aspects of Central European Design." *The Drama Review* 28.2 (Summer 1984): 47-65.

"Josef Svoboda's Scenography for Shakespeare." *Cross Currents 3.* (A Yearbook of Central European Culture) Ed. Ladislav Matejka and Benjamin Stolz. Ann Arbor: University of Michigan Dept. of Slavic Languages and Literatures, 1984: 397-404.

"Svoboda and Vychodil." *Theatre Crafts* 21.8 (October 1987): 34-36ff.

"Josef Svoboda and Laterna Magika's Latest Productions." *Theatre Design and Technology* 24.4 (Winter 1989): 17-27.

THE CHIEF BOOK-LENGTH STUDIES OF SVOBODA IN LANGUAGES OTHER THAN ENGLISH INCLUDE THE FOLLOWING:

Bablet, Denis. *La Scena e L'Imagine.* Turin, Italy: Einaudi, 1970.

_____. *Josef Svoboda.* Lausanne: L'Age d'Homme, 1970. [The French version of the work above.]

Berjozkin, V.J. *Teatr Josefa Svobody.* Moscow: Izdatelstvo Isobrazitelnogo Isskustva, 1973.

Ptáčková, Věra. *Josef Svoboda.* Prague: Divadelní Ústav, 1984.

Schröder, E. and E. Killy. *Josef Svoboda.* Berlin: Akademie der Kunste, 1980.

9

Svoboda in the mid-'60s.

A BRIEF CHRONOLOGY

1920	Born on May 10 in Čáslav, Czechoslovakia
1931-35	Secondary education in Čáslav
1935-38	Apprenticeship and journeyman training in his father's carpentry factory, Čáslav
1938-40	Study at the Masters School of Carpentry, Prague
1940-43	Study at the Special School for Interior Architecture, Prague
1943-45	Instructor of drawing at the apprentice school for woodworking crafts, Prague
1945-51	Study of architecture at the School of Applied and Industrial Arts, Prague
1946-48	Head of design and technical operations at the Theatre of the Fifth of May, Prague
1948-50	Deputy head of design and technical operations at the National Theatre, Prague
1950-70	Head of artistic-technical operations, National Theatre, Prague
1958	First Prize for Laterna Magika at Expo 58 in Brussels; additional awards for specific exhibits: History of Glass, Antenna Switches
1961	First Prize for Foreign Scenography at Biennale in Saõ Paolo, Brazil
1967	London Critics' Award for Best Scenography of 1967
1968	Designated National Artist, Czechoslovakia
1969-1990	Professor of Architecture at the School of Applied and Industrial Arts, Prague
1969	Netherland Sikkens Prize in architecture; also honorary Doctorate, Royal College of Art, London
1970	Los Angeles Critics Award for design of Laurence Olivier's film, *The Three Sisters*
SINCE 1970	Chief scenographer at the National Theatre, Prague
SINCE 1973	Artistic Head of Laterna Magika
1975-80	Technical Consultant at the Grand Theatre, Geneva
1976	American Theatre Association International Theatre Award, New York; Chevalier of Arts and Letters, Paris
1978	Honorary Doctor of Fine Arts, Denison University, Ohio
1984	Honorary Doctor of Fine Arts, Western Michigan University; First Prize in Scenography, Theatre of Europe
1986	Award from United States Institute of Theatre Technology
1987	Honorary Member, Brera Academy of Fine Arts, Milan
1988	Gold Medal for Scenography, Prague Quadriennale
1989	The Royal Industry Designer, London

INTRODUCTION

I may have been twelve or thirteen; it was early spring or late fall—in any case it was nasty outside, cold and damp—and I had a bad sore throat. Although Mother wrapped my neck with cloths filled with heated bran, I felt sick and my only true comfort was the radio by my bedside.

A radio receiver in those days was not nearly as routine as it is today, and although I had previously explored the

assurance that I could be all those things if only I were a good architect.

It's no surprise, therefore, that soon my most admired idols became Michelangelo, Leonardo da Vinci, and all their Renaissance peers. They remain so today because I'm convinced that encoded within them are all the significant meanings of human existence. I was almost forty when I first stood face to face with them in Italy, but I realized that not until that moment had I begun to understand the immortality and infinite possibilities of the human spirit. The Sistine Chapel was just in the process of repair and I was allowed to climb the scaffolding for a close look. And

Svoboda in the mid-1970s in the historic Teatro Olympico, Vicenza, Italy.

device inside out, it was only now that I began to grasp the actual benefits of that magical little box. I didn't feel like reading, so I listened to the radio from morning till night. I enjoyed the feeling that even though I had to stay in bed, I was still being informed about absolutely everything. Those fourteen days of being cut off from the world while still feeling that I had an intimate connection with it left a deep and lasting impression on me.

I heard architecture discussed for the first time on that radio. The lecturer defined architecture as a kind of ground plan of life, which I have believed from that day to this. The lecturer characterized an architect as one who has to know absolutely everything about human activity and life itself. I have always gravitated toward synthesis in everything (even after the most self-destructive analysis). So, at an age when I wanted to be a painter, philosopher, engineer, and even an inventor, chance provided me with the glowing, comforting

there, a little above me, I could see Adam's hand just separating from the fingers of the Creator, as if the spark of life were still quivering between them. I stood thunderstruck at the idea of a painter lying on his back, a candle glued to his forehead, and painting a final version directly into the wet plaster, as if writing his message to future generations. And all the more so in Florence in the Buonorotti Gallery with the torsos of Michelangelo! Never before and never since have I had a more intense feeling of being allowed to participate in the mystery of the origin of a work of art.

The stones that were simultaneously statues revealed not only the intimate dialogue of sculptor and matter, but also his stubborn, often tortured seeking for the heart of that stone. And never have I been more convinced that hidden within every work of art is a force that can allow a person to glimpse the secret of life.

Opposite: Zindel, P. The Effect of Gamma Rays on Man-in-the-Moon Marigolds. National Theatre, Prague, 1972. Dir: J. Pleskot. The literally thousands of spheres that filled most of the space were suspended from the flies; lighting determined the degree to which they were emphasized or subordinated.

SCENOGRAPHY

he designer's participation in production has had the most varied designations. The Germans and we Czechs, following them, have referred to stage "outfitting" (*Ausstattung* or *Výprava*, respectively); in English-speaking countries "stage design" is the usual term; in France, "decoration." These terms reduce a designer's collaboration to "framing" the dramatic work, rather than sharing in its complete creation. But if we consider the experiences and history of Italian theatre and its designers (e.g., Serlio, Palladio, and Galia da Bibiena), we discover that they were joint authors of the theatrical action. Without their

is a real lover of speed. It seems to me that quickness of perception has become a form of aesthetic value for modern man." If this applied that many years ago to painting, it applied and still applies all the more to scenography, which works with kinetic images distributed in space and in the flow of time. Moreover, creative scenography cannot be done for its own sake; you must have fellow workers who have a sense of partnership with scenography.

It's necessary for the entire theatrical team to have a collective perception of space, movement, rhythm, and time during the work's preparation. Several important things take place during this period: the creative shaping of various spaces, and the development of certain relationships—

Offenbach. The Tales of Hoffmann. *Grand Opera of the Fifth of May, Prague, 1946. Dir: Alfred Radok.*

"marvels," drama could not have taken place in its full expressiveness and significance, and Italian theatre would have been the poorer. To render a more precise, more complete, and more meaningful designation of our artistic role, I prefer the term "scenography."

In 1911 Josef Čapek wrote, "The true modern sensibility

between details and the whole, between objects and subjects, between the live, corporeal stage action and perhaps film or other technologies. Without a thorough weighing of such antithetical forces, and without a willing acceptance of assignments by the individual production components, you cannot prepare a production "program."

An effective program always comes about by agreement. The preparation of a theatre production reminds me of an orchestra tuning up. The players must bring their instruments to peak performance level; then the conductor arrives and a unified whole emerges.

I helped to formulate an overall program twice in my life: immediately after the war at the Theatre of the Fifth of May and later at the National Theatre. These programs encompassed only what flowed from the personal

the principle of collage. For example, painted flats were joined with fragile, spatially conceived skeletal constructions, until by degrees there emerged an abstract spatial composition shaped by light. The composition balanced on the very border between an actual object and its painted reproduction. Indeed, some of my early postwar scenic proposals emerged along these lines. For example, *The Tales of Hoffmann* and, later, *The Devil's Wall* employed skeletal constructions in conjunction with painted

Offenbach. The Tales of Hoffmann. *Grand Opera of the Fifth of May, Prague, 1946. Dir: Alfred Radok.*

involvement of all who shared in them. Our fundamental starting point was the awareness that theatre is a collective art.

After the war, we all felt a driving need to continue from where the prewar avant-garde prematurely left off. We wanted to develop their discovery of dramatic space. But concurrent with this linkage to the past, we were already searching for our own new alphabet, namely the laws relating to the movement and transformation of scenography during the flow of dramatic action.

In the formal sense, our work was virtually identical with our prewar models. In principle, however, we shifted our attention from a concern with a coherent whole to its seemingly estranged parts. Further variations then included

pictures; it was, in effect, a near equivalency if not identity of elements.

My work was, of course, not without precedent. When I did my very first serious scenography during the war for *Empedocles*, František Salzer called my work Tairovian. The name meant little to me at that time. I had only a foggy sense of Tairov's theory of an unchained theatre. At the time, Tairov was inaccessible to me, and yet I seemed to absorb his influence.

Just as there is a law of the conservation of energy, there's also a law that the accumulated experiences and discoveries of a given generation produce a certain psychic energy that begins to permeate the culture at large. Through literature and painting, like X-rays, it even reaches people

Gorky. Children of the Sun. *National Theatre, Prague, 1973. Dir: J. Kačer.*

Photo: Jaromír Svoboda

who live in isolation. Nothing is completely lost. And one day the effect of such experiences and discoveries begins to spread like the flow of lava, creating new conventions of seeing and perception for a given age.

In my postwar productions, as well, I must have subconsciously reflected Tairov's conceptions. Of course, there was one fundamental difference. I proceeded to uncouple skeletal construction from pictorial image. I made of them two antithetical elements so contrasting that one denied (in fact, excluded) the other. And if they did create a whole, then it was a distinctly artificial whole. I made no attempt at a synthesis or a homogeneous form. My directorial collaborators in the Theatre of the Fifth of May did exactly the same. They shattered the illusionistic pseudo-coherence of theatre, de-articulated its individual genres, with which we could then freely build, handling them contrapuntally, or merging realities that at first glance seemed incompatible—the past with the present, historical styles with elements of modern civilization. We played out the whole scale of genres from tragedy and grand opera to grotesque farce and fairground frolic. It enabled us to work with the elementary components of theatre and to parody theatre with theatre.[1] Our youthful program was indeed that simple. We were for expressive suggestiveness and against illusionism. Moreover, ours was a theatre of spotlights, not atmospheric, mystic illumination.

It was also generally said of our early work that we drew from impressionism. That, of course, is true; it would be foolish to deny the influence of impressionistic painting. Whatever the school or style of painting might be, scenography has a special, paradoxical, relationship to it.

After all, it's perfectly possible that certain subjects which have the effect of obvious anachronism or anomaly in a painting may become surprisingly authentic and relevant on stage.

Light, for example. The impressionists discovered it for painting, and modern painting subsequently rejected it for its illusionism, but without exhausting all of its possibilities. Light has remained an inexhaustible and unending inspiration for my work.

From the very beginning, I naturally searched, consciously and unconsciously, for my own method of work. Of course, it required self-recognition. For example, I've known for a long time that I work best when time is critically short, when I have to make decisions quickly and definitively. This very risky method depends strictly on feeling and instinct, with thought becoming a spontaneous reflex, as in self-defense. It's like a great improvisation, which would, of course, be an irremediable disaster if it were not backed up by many years of carefully thought through and tenacious work.

Sometimes, perhaps as a reward, you're helped by pure chance, or, perhaps more precisely, a sudden insight, at which point I'm always amazed at how much I didn't see because I was staring too hard. Does the impulse to "insight" come from the outside or has it lain within me for a long time like an unexposed film which developed on its own? All such insights and accidents are, of course, usable only to the extent that they have objective validity at the given moment. Columbus's discovery of America was, according to the Surrealists, an "objective accident." Every banality is full of miracles that can be seen only by one who is able to give them order and form and a logical place in his work.

Giotto wanted to paint the foam on the mouth of a mad dog on one of his frescoes. He tried it ten times, twenty times, and then furiously flung a sponge at the abortive spot. The sponge, soaked with color, created a porous mass of foam on the wall, exactly what the painter had imagined. Or Delacroix. Almost unconsciously he stopped in Saint Sulpice square, flooded in sunshine, and observed a boy climbing the statues in a fountain. Suddenly he became aware of what he was seeing: a dark orange color in the light, the most vivid violet at the edges of the shadows, and golden reflections in the shadows cast on the ground. The orange and the violet alternated, sometimes blended; the golden tone was seemingly tinged with green. He noted this precisely in his diary long before impressionism.

Think of the number of people who strolled the paths of autumnal parks long before the painter who "discovered" rays of sunlight among the branches of the trees and the shifting net of shadows on the ground! It's just that the first impressionist was able to record his vision with the aid of Delacroix's colors, assess the value of the optical perception that maintains our contact with the world, demonstrate the significance of the surface of things, and determine rules for the play of colored and black spots which join on the retina of the eye and become transformed into a final atmospheric, illusionistic form. He thereby solved the puzzle of the changes in colors as they join. I think it's a miracle each time I join blue and yellow pigment on my palette and the result is green. Or when I blend red, green, and blue light from three spotlights aimed so as to overlap each other precisely on a white surface and the result is white.

Even today, I regard the return to the impressionists as logical, not anachronistic, especially in theatre. After all, the greatest problem in theatre from the beginning has been light, form, and movement, which joins them—and those are the primary problems of impressionism. But it's not only a matter of labels; one problem necessarily calls up a second, a third. Moreover, it's possible to learn from completely different, unexpected sources.

For example, Helmholtz, Metzger, and other physicists also thoroughly studied these problems. They established a scale of brightness which we can register optically. They verified the adaptable and apperceptive capabilities of the human eye. They also experimented with color, with perspective, and with optical illusions, as if they were imitating Giorgio Vasari. They alternated red squares with gray ones—and the red squares seemed to come forward, whereas the sides of the squares, placed at a diagonal, seemed to collapse.

The human eye can estimate the absolute size of an illuminated surface only with difficulty. It is far better at estimating the contrast between the illumination of two neighboring surfaces or the contrast of two separate illuminations, one after the other.

Impressionism has within it links to the Baroque, to romanticism, to illusionism, and so on. But it is also the beginning of modern art because it is precisely in impressionism that, after a long interval, art begins to collaborate with science once again.

This union of art and science is essential and vitally necessary for our time. It provides art with a rational basis and helps us to carry our investigations further. If I need a cylinder of light on stage with a dispersion of less than one degree at its base, I need to gather an entire scientific and technical team to construct such a cylinder. Only with such a team were we able to put together a hollow cylinder of light for *Tristan and Isolde* in Cologne in 1969.[2]

The same approach was necessary for experiments with variations of mirror reflections or sculpturesque effects by means of lighting. At the time I worked mainly with white, daytime light. I was concerned with its form; I worked with it as if it were a substance, a mass. When I wanted a figure to disappear suddenly from the stage, I needed to solve the technical question of how to turn spotlights on and off as quickly and precisely as a shot from a rifle. We furnished the spotlights with shutters of the kind that are found in cameras, and we established their most effective exposure at one-fifth of a second. None of these discoveries resulted from caprice, nor did we solve any task in an offhand manner. The reason was always dramatic necessity.

In 1958 I was asked the question on a survey, "Does modern technology belong in modern theatre in the same way that an elevator belongs in a modern house?" I thought the question was posed entirely incorrectly. Whether or not technology belongs in theatre isn't an issue at all—there can be no doubt that it does—but what function does it have in it, and how does it function in the dramatic work? And you can't answer that with a formula.

Some eras have searched for formulas, needless to say without success. It is perhaps already clear that you can't do

Kundera. The Owners of the Keys.
National Theatre, Prague, 1962.
Dir: Otomar Krejča.
The hallucinatory scenes employed a square mirror that reflected the extremely intense lights aimed at it from the proscenium's inner borders.

Photo: Jaromír Svoboda

static theatre, in which scenery rigidly gazes down on actions played out within its space. After all, what is actually fixed in the stream of life? Is a room in which someone declares love the same as a room in which someone is dying? By the same token, a summer pond with an unending horizon is not transformed solely by the atmosphere of the day, but primarily by the gaze of those who stand on its shores. Gordon Craig once explained it in a note that actually foreshadowed his design drama, *The Stairs*: "Have you ever been in love and had the feeling that the street before you suddenly expands, that houses grow, sing, lose themselves, and it seems to you that the street darkens drastically, levitates, and becomes transformed into a cloud? In reality you were walking along an ordinary street—or so everyone claims, but it's a lie, don't believe them, keep faith in your own truth, which is the truth of ecstasy."

But we are able to perceive truth and understand it only

17

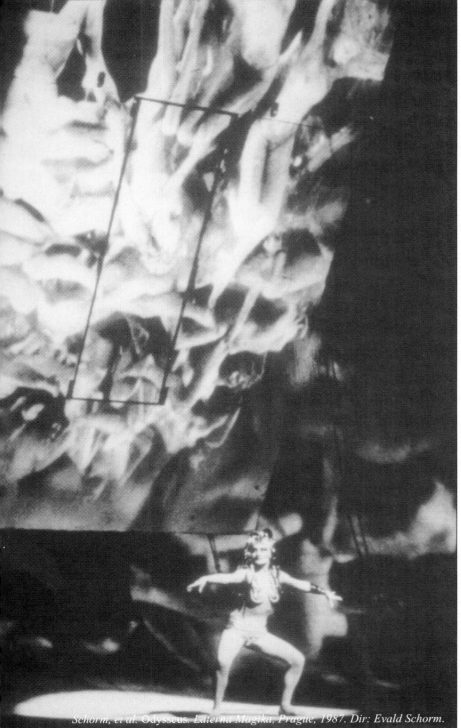

Schorm, et al. Odysseus. Laterna Magika, Prague, 1987. Dir: Evald Schorm.

In other words, there's more truth and honesty in conscious artifice than in a traditional illusion of reality.

At the Theatre of the Fifth of May we knew it was possible to fabricate most everything on stage, but we nevertheless avoided any products of nature. The possibilities for creating illusion on the stage aren't nearly as great as the neorealistic aesthetic of the 1930s believed. Moreover, such possibilities certainly don't remain stable; they vary according to eras. Actually, theatre from its very origin has been coping with the dilemma of illusionism and anti-illusionism. The inclination toward one or the other pole always meant a change in style.

John Philip Kemble and Charles Kean staked everything on stage machinery and illusionistic spectacle, while in reaction to them the anti-illusionistic movement fought for the rehabilitation of Shakespeare under the leadership of Karl Zimmermann, the creator of the Shakespearean stage of fixed architecture, inspired by Renaissance models. And the result? Anti-illusionism was shown to be only a seeming antithesis, especially if we view it through the eyes of an actor forced to play in an historically accurate but "mute" surrounding which neither supported him nor established active contact with him.

And we can continue the dialectic from Antoine and Stanislavsky to their antitheses in the constructivists, Craig, and the designers of the Bauhaus. However paradoxical it may sound, antitheses can be antitheses only when they have at least one point of contact in common. Otherwise they miss each other entirely. In fact, placing illusionism and anti-illusionism into opposition is entirely pointless. The measure of this mistake is the actor. An anti-illusionistic stage compels him to represent everything the stage itself is unable to represent; it compels him to strengthen illusionism. After all, the actor is the single indispensable element of theatre; he carries within him the potential and the necessity for his transformation into a dramatic character, the basic element of illusionism.

I know all this today. But I was once an anti-illusionist, and then an illusionist; now I'd rather speak of suggestion, which is their point of contact, suggestion based on transformation. And that's where I see the fundamental difference between the old illusionistic theatre and today's theatre. I'm not interested in making a burning bush or an erupting volcano on stage, in creating an illusion of reality, but in acknowledging the reality of theatrical elements, which can be transformed nonmaterially into almost anything. I've called them "space in space." For years this possibility of infinite transformation has fascinated me, as has the search for the real, authentic, and inherent reality of the stage.

The stage floor, the proscenium arch, the ceiling, and the relationship of stage and audience space—these function merely as determinants of dramatic space, its external resources that define it and demarcate it optically. But what is played out within this space? No one became more thoroughly involved with these problems than Vlastislav Hofman. At the time when his work was peaking, he solved them with obvious urgency in the dramatization of Dostoyevsky's *Crime and Punishment* and *The Idiot*, as well as in Solochov's *Distressed Earth*. Hofman revealed

under certain circumstances. I constantly and stubbornly have tried to gauge the disproportion of forces between the artificial reality of theatre and "real" reality; an actual construction juxtaposed to the background of "artificially" painted trees in *The Devil's Wall* or the photomontage in *The Tales of Hoffmann*; stereometric forms and film projection (more precisely a kinetic montage) in *Astray*; mobile Renaissance architecture with a landscape painting placed at its center in the 1954 production of *Rigoletto*. All of these attempts have one thing in common—artifice, emphatic artifice as a foundation for the building of a scenic image. Such consciously contrived "illusion" can never result in disillusionment and reveal the falseness of things.

Nezval. Today the Sun Still Sets on Atlantida. *National Theatre, Prague, 1956. Dir: Alfred Radok.*

Photo: Jaromír Svoboda

the side section of structures and doubled the proscenium arch, thereby doubly emphasizing that transparent wall stretched across the proscenium arch, behind which the dramatic characters live as though unseen. In so doing, he posed the question of space in space in its most elemental form, although it would remain a question of static space.

In Vítezslav Nezval's play *Today the Sun Still Sets on Atlantida* (1956), I added a secondary black proscenium arch graphically reinforced by horizontal lines in perspective to create what seemed to be a second stage terminated by an obviously painted cyclorama. In *The Queen of Spaces* (1976), two scrim surfaces inclined toward each other, with a transparent opening into farther space. One of these surfaces, covered with projected drapery, functioned as a ceiling, the second as a raked floor, even though it was not congruent with the actual stage floor. I talk about this problematical matter in such detail in order to make it clear that I never forgot that a proscenium stage has a floor, a portal (that is, a proscenium arch), and ceiling, and that these are its only real elements—this is also why I always use them as my starting point. In the understanding

of these three realities lies the secret of dramatic and production space.

I've always been an advocate of the proscenium stage because it is the most theatrical space available; moreover, the routine transformation of theatre into mere spectacle isn't readily possible in it. Although neither the National Theatre in Prague nor most European theatres are suitable places for experiment or for truly modern theatre—for a fully satisfying interplay of all components or essential progress in basic elements, like light and sound—one simply has to take their form into account and put new elements into old containers. Europe won't be tearing down its historic theatres, nor will it build new theatres in large numbers, and so we have to keep seeking new variations for the functions of old theatre space—at least until a new space is created, as I shall suggest.

Dramatic space has the same characteristics as a poetic image. Its inseparable property is the fictional space of an imaginary stage that reaches beyond the physical stage in all directions. Dramatic space is protean in its mutability of size and identity. Opposing this dynamic space, then, is the

19

Photo: Jaromír Svoboda

Sophocles. Oedipus-Antigone.
Theatre Beyond the Gate, Prague, 1971.
Dir: Otomar Krejča.
*The wooden cubes rode in on rails and were
also suspended from overhead tracks.*

actual, static theatre space, functional space, whose specific type is determined by the relation of stage and audience: proscenium space, central space, thrust space, variable space. So-called new types of space are merely imprecise reconstructions of historical prototypes—imprecise because of their almost inevitable placement indoors, if for no other reason.

Theatre space has been deprived of imaginative power, of an uninterrupted freeing of the spectator's fantasy. Should the border between stage and audience continue to be strictly maintained, or is it possible to do away with this division and situate the production within a single undivided space, in which—in extreme cases—there might be an indiscriminate mixing of actors and spectators? It seems to me we are constantly groping around a cursed concept, "theatre" space.

If a characteristic of theatre is the act of transformation, which converts a stage into a dramatic space, an actor into a dramatic character, and a visitor into a spectator, then even theatre space, architectonically speaking, must achieve a higher qualitative level and be transformed. After all, it's not a matter of theatre space, but of the space for a production, therefore production space, and that is fundamentally different from theatre space.

Theatre space is a familiar schema, to which a production is supposed to subordinate itself even at the cost of becoming deformed. And if we continue to be preoccupied merely with theatre space, we'll be solving something that in its very foundation is not concrete. We'll be trying to modernize an old architectonic type with new external elements, without ever touching the real heart of the problem. Production space, on the other hand, gets its dimensions from the dramatic work and its inner forces—time, rhythm, movement, suggestion, intangible energy. Though intangible, they are nevertheless real, in the way sound waves determine the curved contour of a concert hall.

Production space is a place of conflict, and the static nature of theatre, inherited from tradition, is no longer acceptable. Proscenium space is only one of the possible spatial configurations of production space, as the amphitheatre of antiquity or the Elizabethan theatre were other restrictive variants. That's why there are so many difficulties with Shakespearian texts, which, if put on our stages, undergo an act of forced deformation. Equally hard to solve is the problem of staging ancient or medieval drama, because our contemporary theatre admits only a few specific design approaches and their repetition in more or less novel variations.

An atelier-theatre, which, as I see it, I'll no longer succeed in building, would be an architectonically neutral space and would make possible a different relationship between audience and stage for every production. Its ground plan would be a rectangle, surrounded by galleries on several levels, connected in the corners by vertical communication systems. These galleries would have several functions; they would serve the technical operations of lighting and projections as well as the entrances of actors; and if the production were taking place on the entire stage floor level of production space, the galleries could be used to seat spectators. By moving these galleries along their transverse axes you could change the proportions of the rectangle of production space. Most of the spectators would be seated on mobile seating units, each one holding about one hundred people, which would move on cushions of air and be easily arranged around the performance areas and readily change their angle of seating. And all this could be done *during* the course of the play. If the nature of a given play required it, the collective seating modules could in fact be removed from the audience area with the spectators or without them and return again when needed. (Not to mention what an ideal security measure they would be in the event of a fire.)

Even the foyer could be included as a parallel dramatic or supplemental space, by installing in it an exhibit of pictures relevant to the play being done, or by playing certain kinds of recorded music, and so on.

The fly space would be located in an optimal part of the production space. The proscenium towers and bridges would not be fixed, so that the proscenium portal could have a variety of forms and dimensions; it wouldn't always have to be parallel with a frontal axis; it could be eliminated entirely. The stage traps would also serve as elevators for transporting stage pallets for individual productions as well as for special pallets—for instance, a small pool, or a turntable. The stage traps would lead to special storage spaces which would be connected to the scenographic and costume shops in which the entire production would receive its finishing touches. Otherwise, the specialized theatre workshops, as well as the central storage spaces, would be located at sites other than the atelier. I would not complicate the stage floor with traditional heavy stage machinery; instead, I would make use of light, mechanized scenographic components.

Scenography makes sense only when it becomes an instrument in the hands of a director, when it becomes a space for inspiration, a kind of technical and design plaything. Production space should be a kind of piano, on which it is possible to improvise, to test out any idea whatever, or to experiment with the relationship among various components. Only so, by means of concrete experiment, is it possible for everyone's words and creative ideas to share the same objective reality.

This new technology in the new studio ought not to flaunt itself. The spectator should be unaware of it, just as he is when watching a magician perform his magic.

And theatre *ought* to be a place of magic. Nothing from life can be transferred intact into the theatre; we must always create a theatrical reality and then fill it with the dynamics of life In that principle lies one of the essences of modern art. There was a time when I considered Mallarmé's graphic poems and Apollinaire's calligraphy as mere games to fill empty hours. And yet they represented the highest possible efforts towards a purification of elements, towards a rejection of conventional expressive accretions, towards an artistic evolution in the direction of synthesis. These were precisely chosen, deliberate words revealing an economy suggesting that the words were to be carved in stone tablets but were instead broken up into letters arranged in a graphic pictorial layout. A picture confronted, completed, and heightened by words—or words heightened

course, every phenomenon—if it is not to be a mere static fact—must be observed in the flow of time. And time is expressed through change. Not mechanical change, but change as the flowing current of a lively imagination, like the clouds above a landscape that never acquire substance, never become a solid spatial form. Inspiration came from music, from Proust, and from Bergson. This special perception of change—as a fluid current—was taken as its own by the visual symphony of film, and taken as its own even by theatre. We, too, adopted this image of an unbroken stream, but we replaced its coherence with changeable and variously oriented layers so that its flow on the stage did not become monotonous, so that it could be modified in order to

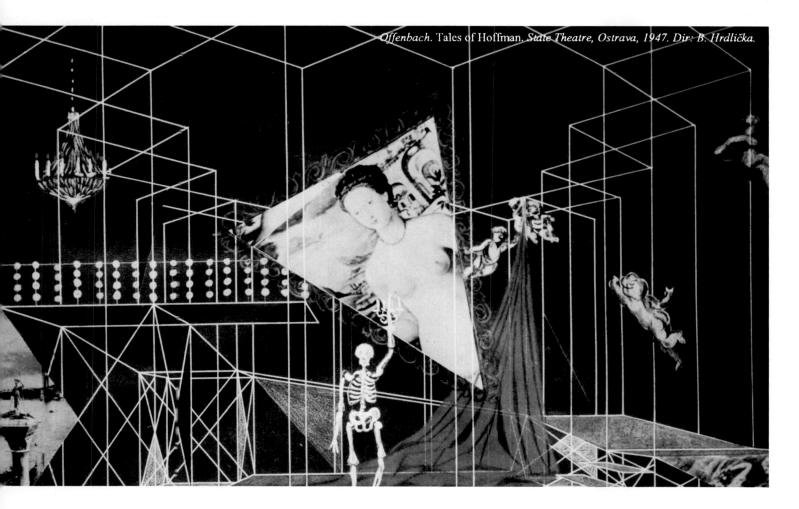

Offenbach. Tales of Hoffman. State Theatre, Ostrava, 1947. Dir: B. Hrdlička.

by form. This evolution of word as well as of form resulted in a still further significance. Purification—the tendency toward simplification and elimination of non-essentials— is one of the typical and general signs of modern art. I followed it intensely in the hope that by this path I might arrive at a true synthesis of essential elements in new relationships.

The basic difference between the synthetic theatre of the '30s and our efforts at the end of the '50s and '60s was in fact right here: E.F. Burian, for example, wanted to achieve synthesis by erasing the boundaries between individual arts, to create a new homogeneous form from analytically dispersed elements. We, on the other hand, insisted on a purity of discrete elements, with their impressionistic union to be completed in the eye and mind of the spectators. Of

mesh with the tripartite nature of time—its past, present, and future, which, indeed, found their point of intersection on our stage.

And we are back to theatre space, polyscenic space. But polyscenic-ness does not merely mean simultaneity or the indication of several actions occurring concurrently in several distinct places. Polyscenic-ness is an expression of a free and many-sided time-space operation, in which one and the same action is observed from several optical and ideational angles which set cause and effect next to each other and take their measure. Polyscenic-ness means a visible joining and severing of these "axes," these relationships—a breaking up of the linear continuity of a theatre action, and its transformation into separate events or moments.

Photo: Josef Svoboda

Mozart. Idomeneo. *National Arts Center, Ottawa, 1981. Dir: Václav Kašlık.*

But any process, if it is to be perceivable, must be divided into definite, deliberate cycles with a precise rhythm. And so one day we found ourselves considering the problem of pauses, intermissions, breaks of whatever kind in the flow of action, which are as necessary in theatre as they are in music, where rests are as necessary as notes; rests are instruments of articulation in that they help organize and emphasize musical patterns. In theatre, if a pause has a precisely calculated length, it can heighten dramatic tension and become a dramatic fact. The effectiveness of pauses depends, of course, on their placement in the current of the action, and also on their frequency. Therefore, we carefully placed pauses where they would dramatically reinforce coherence. As a result, drama stopped being a condition and became a process. Time and rhythm acquired a precise, almost tangible quality. And I suddenly realized the true sense of Paul Klee's assertion: "Art should not picture the visible, but make the invisible visible, which means that it must translate the world into new pictorial laws or principles. Instead of the phenomenon of a tree, brook, or rose, we are more interested in revealing the growth, flow, and blossoming which takes place within them."

Klee's observation should apply to theatre as well, if it wants to be a valid art of the twentieth century. An effective rhythm of the dramatic process arises from alternating the complex and the simple, and in revealing the complexity beneath a simple surface. But all this would be pointless if this process weren't capable of resonating in the consciousness of the spectator. If we did not believe in this resonance and sense of identification between spectator and dramatic action, we would have to give up hope of even partially revealing what art is, and instead pursue mere cultural education. If our work is to have meaning, we must count on having an equal partner in our public. We depend on spectators to whom we don't have to explain the story of Romeo and Juliet, of Hamlet, because they all know it.

It's necessary, then, not merely to illustrate a literary text, but to transform it creatively into specific theatrical elements. It means adding to the triad of *Fact-Sign-Emotional convention* the direct joining of facts and emotional conventions, the expression of which we used to call a "ceremony," specifically, a familiar folk ceremony.

The goal of our creative work was always elementary theatre, nothing but the simplest of simplicities. Radok always rejuvenated ceremonies; he wanted to create new embodiments for them, which would be vital and communicable at any given moment. I recall, for example, how the maids in the *House of Bernarda Alba* (1967) scrubbed the floor and set up the chairs. They touched them and sat on them for a moment, the way people do when working. At that moment they were suddenly transformed into a still life in a portrait studio. The setting for this drama, in which even a bell and a voice were gestures, had to have a precise demarcation within the white walls of a black house. The walls didn't merely demonstrate that the house is isolated from the rest of the world; they played an important and active role in the acoustics of the performance. Acoustics must prove as malleable as spatial proportions or projected images. Steps and work noises were produced with great fidelity and precisely graded intensity. The sound of hate and dissension was captured in the crash of an ironbound wooden bucket against the wooden gate of the stable. Precisely at that moment the director suspended the dialogue and let the sound of the metal—this nonverbal "speech"—resonate to its end. He also used sound to reinforce the piercing of Martirio's palm by a needle in order to evoke an image of blood and hatred. The space had to provide a different "coloration" to the sound of the steps which walked the house at night, a different one to the singing of harvesters returning from the fields, and another to the sound of the people from the village.

The walls could muffle and deflect every sound from their interior as well as intensify or emphasize disturbing sounds from without. With lighting, the walls could acquire an expressive texture or become instantly smooth. Interacting with lighting and the actor, they could create a particularly striking effect: a figure pressed against the wall and illuminated by increasingly intense rays of light falling next to her began to darken. When a white rectangle of light is projected onto a gray surface, the rest of the surface optically darkens. In *Bernarda Alba* I merely chose the opposite approach.

At other times, I was faced with the problem of moving large objects on stage. How to avoid having the orchestration of such movements seem mechanical, insufficiently variable, or merely repetitive even when they were fundamental and any changes would be impossible, unthinkable without them? The worst that can happen is the breakdown of available resources when you try to do too much at once: for example, projections, the movement of objects, plus the imposition of external details. It's always necessary to establish from the start a definite principle of restriction, to make the scenery and the furniture

Verdi. Rigoletto. *Smetana Theatre, Prague, 1954. Dir: Bohumil Hrdlička.*

Wagner. Tristan and Isolde. *Grand Theatre, Geneva, 1978. Dir: Jean-Claude Riber.*

Photo: Jaroslav Svoboda

Rostand. Cyrano de Bergerac. *National Theatre, Prague, 1974. Dir: M. Macháček.*

Vishnevsky, V. Optimistic Tragedy. *National Theatre, Prague, 1975. Dir: M. Macháček.*

Photo: Jaroslav Svoboda

homogeneous elements, capable of disappearing at the right moment. It's also essential to weigh minutely the significance of the setting's every detail, which means starting with the detail and finally returning to reappraise it with the whole in mind. This is the only way to be certain that the whole is properly composed in its larger strokes.

I often begin with a simple drawing to capture an "image" of the scene with a mere few lines. The result is a caricature-like abbreviation, emphasizing the characteristic features of a scene. Such a drawing will reveal the excessive details that can infiltrate a dramatic production. And it's just this abundance and excessiveness that you must guard against, whether its source is the author's stage directions, the director's concept, or the producer's bias. You mustn't merely fulfill commissions and try to please. You must stubbornly search for what all the elements have in common, what is possible to unify in an eloquent but still

even lead to a paradoxical situation in which suddenly and unexpectedly a quality emerges that was seemingly negated by this spontaneous process. In theatre no one has, nor will ever have, the luxury of testing his experiment safely in a laboratory where it is possible to undo mistakes. Before the war, experiments occurred mostly in small semi-professional theatres, in front of an audience prepared for experiments. Only from there were such experiments, already tested, adopted into the established theatres. After the war, it was the complete opposite: experiments took place on the large stage of the Theatre of the Fifth of May and then in the National Theatre; only afterward did they travel to provincial theatres, often, unfortunately, as foolish imitations irrelevant to the plays at hand. Contrary to all rules, quality changed into quantity.

There was a fashionable wave of multiple projection screens and curtains of light, of shadow images behind

Chekhov. The Sea Gull. *Theatre Beyond the Gate, Prague, 1972. Dir: Otomar Krejča.*

single form. Of course, I am writing of that stage of my work which would be impossible without the prior experiences with Laterna Magika. (See chapter on "Laterna Magika.")

Experiment in the theatre is the same as intervention into a living organism. Such experiment or intervention never occurs in the isolation of a single element. It prompts movement in the entire structure, and the reaction and its extent are unpredictable. The start of one of my experiments was the idea of a rubbery imitation of grillwork; the end was the reality of a wall that could be walked through, composed of droplets of water. Intermediate steps involved experiments with gas and a screen of light. A logical evolution led from one step to the other almost according to physical laws, but an unexpected by-product appeared: a black floor began to look gray under intense light, which in turn prompted the need to create a grate-like surface to restore its black appearance. That led to lighting from below, but lighting from below resulted in a problem of reflection... Something like a chain reaction begins, in which everything shifts, new relations are created, new forms of the most varied elements. Such chain reactions can

proscenium arches spanned with scrim, of blue triangles on the cyclorama or stairs cutting through the stage floor to lead into the orchestra pit, as if Vlastislav Hofman hadn't already given stairs a definitively precise spatial form and a precise dramatic function. Then various constructions of raw wood took the place of stairs. Fashion or modishness simply doesn't have a logical evolution; perhaps it doesn't have any evolution at all. It has no goal in the future; it's a mere shifting of tastes. But the vagaries of fashion can never be an argument against experiment, because they are two completely different phenomena.

The postwar period has had an opposite evolutionary direction from the past. Postwar scenic experiment correlated with the condition and potential of technology existing outside the theatre. It could grow only from a strong economic foundation, from a wide circle of collaborators and from financial security, which enabled experiment to achieve at least a relative degree of definition and finish. In short, experiment today requires more than paper, burlap, paints, a ladder, and enthusiasm unsupported by knowledge and exactness. Traces of dilettantism must also be eliminated from the final form because the technical element of experiment, like a sudden burst of light, reveals

Garcia-Lorca. The House of Bernarda Alba. *Schlosspark Theater, Berlin, 1966. Dir: Alfred Radok. The Prague production occurred a year later.*

Photo: Ilse Buhs

every imperfection and lack of precision.

Yet, despite all these basic requirements, our theatre at home lacks the basic investment principles for any sort of experiment. Everything I've ever done has in fact been borrowed from exhibitions, prolonging the exhibitions' short-term investments into theatrical life. That's why I worked on Laterna Magika and on Polyekran. I could never have actualized either on a theatre budget. But as soon as exhibitions themselves became repetitious I stopped doing them. As far as Laterna Magika is concerned, we try to squeeze the most from what we have, but unless someone in authority realizes that it's impossible to keep this sort of operation running for thirty years on the basis of its initial outfitting, we'll be forced to end even Laterna Magika.[3]

Scenography has always lived from borrowings, which isn't so bad. What's worse is that it still lacks a basic registration of its resources, something which is routine in technology and which Bertolt Brecht strove for in his day.

A registration, which would certainly not lead to a stylistic norm, would bring into scenography a sense of system, which always goes hand in hand with economy—economy not only in terms of finances but also time; above all, however, in terms of artistic effect, of quality. Filmmakers and television workers immediately grasp every technical improvement; they count on it. As soon as it became possible, they started to work with color, stereophonic sound, wide angle images, and montage effects. Meanwhile, in the theatre, we have a constant, inexplicable confusion of technical elements with artistic elements. Stage designers are forced into a never-ending process of discovery and simultaneous suppression of their discoveries. Why? Merely to satisfy contemporary demands for "art" and originality at any price. No one seems to realize that such an unending process, at a minimum, limits the possibility of thinking through any experiment and giving it systematic validity.

Of course, every new technical element represents only a fragment of the technical foundation needed by all

26

moments the wall became transparent, at other times it functioned as a mirror or as a projection surface on which a character would see himself, his own image evoked by memories and the way he imagined himself to be. The interplay of these three elements—the glass wall, its almost imperceptible movement, and light—obviated any need for a separate abstract image to communicate an impression of space.

The greatest problem of a mirror on stage is to be there when it's needed, and disappear once it fulfills its task. The glass wall, which reflected a person, even made it possible to see behind the wall and also to project images which wiped out the mirroring effect.

No designer is subject to as much pressure and restriction as a scenographer. His fate is to wait. He does not have the possibility of free choice as a painter or sculptor does. A theme is simply given to him and he must subordinate himself to it. It's like pressure from opposing directions: the ideas that he wants to embody, and the ideas that he must embody. If the aesthetic function dominates in most design areas, in stage design it takes second place to practical function, to serving the play and the actors, serving the overall dramatic quality. And at the same time, the scenographer must be preparing himself for his future work; he can't allow himself to wait to solve problems until the moment he is thrust before them.

The relation between direction and scenography is extraordinarily important; more precisely, between the director and the scenographer. I always try to take into account all the human characteristics of my partner, his inventiveness as well as his reactions, if we come to a conflict of attitudes or opinions. Collaboration usually involves two contrasting phases: the work on the production and the climate after its conclusion. A production appears before the public as a fact to be responded to in and of itself, without regard to its past, its possibility of further development, or the separate contributions of its creators. If we are not aware of the evolution of a production, how can we recognize where the work of one creative component ends and where the work of another begins, where one exceeds the other, where direction penetrates into scenography and the opposite?

In the first phase of a collaboration there has to be a mutual interest in the production, a desire to give it one's best. In the second phase human nature begins to dominate, and sometimes a director may perhaps even decide to do without scenography in the next production. Working for so many years in the theatre, I've come to view this cycle as a necessity, so as to be able to explain the waves which alternate between an emphasis on scenography and its suppression. These waves repeat themselves almost regularly, and their reasons don't really change very much. They include a certain inner movement within art, as well an inner movement of human, social tendencies to which art is exposed. In 1948 we worked out the question of the relation of scenography and direction for the first time, at the end of the '50s for the second time, at the end of the '60s for the third time. The issue emerges with almost mathematical regularity every ten years. The reasons need not be merely feelings of competition, but also a

scenographers. People, presumably in the interest of theatre, take up arms against its industrialization, to which experiment allegedly leads. No one speaks of a fear of theatrical dilettantism! But it is impossible for theatre to remain totally behind in technical advancements without becoming a museum.

What is the source of the conflicting attitudes regarding technology and its function in theatre? Most people see technology only in terms of machinery. I went through this phase myself. In its essence, however, theatre technology is active and capable of dramatic action, even when that technology is "non-technical." In fact, I've come to the conclusion that technology can even be intangible, as it was, for example, in the production of Gombrowicz's *The Wedding* (1958). Its changes of locale, their thorough-going transformation, could never be accomplished by theatrical machinery—traps, flies, turntables, moving belts, and wagons. For the required dream-like distortion of reality I used glass walls placed at a diagonal on the stage. At certain

Gombrowicz. The Wedding. *Schiller Theatre, Berlin, 1968. Dir: Ernst Schröder.*

subconscious need to create a truthful accounting of results, to audit the mutual relations among individual components with an eye to their further potential, and to orient oneself in the evolution to come.

It can even come to a denial of scenography—theoretically—not in practice, unless theatre for some incomprehensible reason wishes to self-destruct. It's enough to think of one good example, say from Orson Welles' *The Trial*: a huge waiting room in a railroad station, and somewhere in the middle of it a desk and chair. An office. I challenge anyone to express this atmosphere, its basic feeling, as immediately, concentratedly, and essentially by any means other than those of a stage setting. Any means other than those of scenography simply don't exist.

And still another conceptual point: if a given work is to contain diametrically opposing and uninterchangeable thematic elements, a way must still be found to join such elements at a deeper level. For a production of Richard Strauss's *Die Frau Ohne Schatten* at Covent Garden in 1967, I made thirty scenic proposals, thirty illustrations of almost imperceptible and yet undeniably existing aesthetic laws. And somehow they all related to human nature, even though I wasn't fully aware of it. *Die Frau Ohne Schatten* is a fable of a person who sold her soul and with it her humanity. As in every fable, the world of good and the world of evil are thrust into direct contrast.

But what form and what color do good and evil have and how are they related? Just as I was searching for the right form and color for the scene, so its principles began forming almost on their own, without my interference and often against my will. Signs of duality appeared in my proposals sooner than I was able to realize their implications or define them. Finally, a whole emerged, a circle, broken into two parts which obviously belonged together even though they were placed so as to touch like two half-circles only at the midpoint of their circumference. It was a circle and a whole which ceased being a whole but became two separate parts without denying their mutual affinity. Then I proceeded to add stairs to these half-circles and created from them two acting areas that touched at a sharp angle—the kings' space and the space of Barak's workshop. The latter was placed under the lower slab and its interior was revealed when the lower segment lifted up. At the same time, this entire scenic construction was not a symbol, nor did it function as a symbol. In fact, it was merely a scrap of the play, a resonance of its idea cleansed of all details, something the play itself couldn't say in as elegant an abbreviation. It was something only a designer can express.

The play itself ended with this simplified image. But I still had a further, essential problem. Barak and his wife, rid of her shadow, stood confronting each other on a diagonal, because a spatial diagonal is optically the greatest achievable distance on a stage. And this distance was

Strauss. Die Frau Ohne Schatten. *Royal Opera, London, 1967. Dir: R. Hartmann.*

suddenly spanned by a shadow like a bridge across a chasm, like the touch of a hand. The spectator could see both the substance and the intangibility of a shadow which one could walk across. It used to be common practice to have a real bridge in this scene. I wanted a real shadow. But how to do it? If a character stood on a mirrored surface and was illuminated, the shadow would be lost. It would be a strange vision of the world, the kind one sees in a Van Gogh picture. And that was my starting point for solving the problem. But a mirrored stage floor ruled out any sort of projection, which I needed for my type of leaf-shaped projection screens. Moreover, a mirrored floor when illuminated would have been transformed into such a strong reflecting surface that the torrent of light would have flooded the entire stage. And on top of that, an entire mirrored floor made it impossible to lose and regain a shadow, which was understandably essential for the whole play. It didn't even allow for two people to stand next to each other and have one of them be shadowless. At the same time, the play of shadows had to be distinctive and actual; there was no room here for any sort of "let's pretend." The problem was like the dangerous reefs inherent in the dual roles of a designer and a director.

To create the first type of shadow (the "bridge"), it was enough to install a system of black venetian blind shutters in the risers of the stairs. But in addition to this gigantic shadow I needed an instrument which could instantly create an actual shadow and in another instant eliminate it. The only resource with this capability is light and the surface it strikes: a combination of diffused light from below a special flooring with strong, sharply aimed lighting above. The lower light, aimed up toward the fly space in which it

disappeared without creating parasitic light or weakening the intensity of any projections, passed through a grating of black steel strips laid at right angles to each other, on whose sufficiently wide edges the actors were able to walk. The shadows cast by the upper light were caught on the vertical surfaces of the grating and could be wiped out at any moment by the light from below. In effect, a floor of this sort of grating cannot become gray from intensive lighting, as happened to me with the black carpet in Tyl's *Drahomira*; on the contrary, the greater the intensity of the lighting, the darker this floor became.

As far as the leaf-shaped screens were concerned, I had never realized how difficult it is to paint any abstract form other than a geometric one. A vegetative form always seems to suggest reality, even if that reality suggests something like a coral cliff or an amoeba. But a projected geometric image didn't blend well with a vegetative screen. The screen didn't give the projected image a form but was merely its passive carrier; it was covered and disappeared under it. The most we had was a contact but never an interplay of deliberately shaped surfaces, even though a vegetative screen actually facilitates a spatial interplay. With these screens I was also able to verify some elementary rules of design for the stage, such as the interaction of colored abstract composition on a textured surface.

All my life I've asked myself questions: Why is it necessary to project only onto solid surfaces and not onto a mobile cluster of lines, on fragmentary

Svoboda adjusts his model for Shakespeare's Midsummer Night's Dream
*(National Theatre, Prague, 1963. Dir: V. Špidla) at an exhibition of his
work at the University of Michigan, Ann Arbor, in 1981.*

surfaces, or on sticks or rods? Why isn't it possible to introduce light into their layers as well as onto their surface? I experimented with the possibility of the permeability of two projected images which intersected in space, struck each other at a right angle, and one literally penetrated the other. I tested further possibilities of additive colored lighting. I attempted to construct a light-absorbing device. I have spent my life searching for new and newer solutions and progressively revealed their possibilities and limitations. Let me repeat that a scenographer mustn't allow himself to solve tasks only at the moment he is standing in front of them; they will surely outrun his unprepared thinking and knowledge. I simply don't believe in genius that can instantly adapt to any problem whatever.

I do believe in the results of an ability to perceive events and activity around one, in the ability to gather within oneself the most varied information and stimuli and to use them at the appropriate moment. Moreover, I'm convinced that no problems can be handled by merely walking around their edges; it is necessary to penetrate to their essence even at the cost of temporary destruction or negation, which may even be a necessary antipole and consequence of any attempt to configurate space.

I have in mind an empty stage. (I am convinced that it's always necessary to start from that which is normally thought to be nothing, because that sort of "nothing" on stage simply doesn't exist.) Stage space is a fact that exists in and of itself prior to the play and outside the play. And perhaps that is the fundamental problem: to make of that space an empty space. It's far more difficult than erecting a normal setting. And then, to make an empty space, perhaps a blue space. Nothing more. I emphasize "to make" because it's possible to take a board and cover it with black paint, but it's also possible to take that same board and make of it a painting which will be called "Black Paint." It's exactly the same with space. Color is a reality and space is a reality, and it is doubly so with dramatic space.

And so, indeed, I have always kept returning, searching, and disputing with myself; there have been but very few brief moments when I have had the feeling that I knew something precisely. But one thing I truly know well: the stage is an instrument, as perfect an instrument as a piano. An instrument on which it is possible to play Chopin, and the stars will fall from the heavens; or Beethoven, and grief will acquire form and substance; or Mahler, or Orff, or Gershwin. On stage it is possible to play anything. And play it beautifully.

Strauss. Die Frau Ohne Schatten. *Royal Opera, London, 1967. Dir: R. Hartmann.*

Opposite: Janáček. The Voyages of Mr. Brouček *National Theatre, Prague, 1959.
Photo: Jaromír Svoboda*

’m always surprised at how many great moments and events in life I've forgotten (did they actually occur?); and in contrast how many trivial moments I remember as if they happened yesterday. Memory, our own inner computer, knows what's most essential to us and automatically registers what is truly most important.

I remember a certain visit to grandmother in the country in cherry picking time. Little balls of cherries shone in the fields, especially along those which—carved into the terrain—followed its rolling waves. Once, unobserved, I stood at the edge of a small cherry orchard in which my uncle was cultivating trees. The image of a solitary orchard keeper, whose hands lovingly touch small branches as if they're conversing together, the image of an individual and nature at the moment they're mutually sharing secrets, has always stayed with me, as has the image of fields of rye and sugar beets, and childish curiosity about what might be happening in the middle of a hidden world with its little

Karnet. Astray. *Municipal Theatre,.Prague, 1944. Dir: František Salzer. Not produced. This is a model built many years later.*

tops of leafy trees and in baskets all around us. Our entire family sat at a wooden table covered with a linen tablecloth and ate white rye bread and butter, which lay on sugar beet leaves. I no longer recall what we talked about, but through it all I had a blissful feeling of our togetherness. And I saw how the trees, not too thickly leafed, cast a strange shadow. When I later met the Impressionists, and still much later when I was doing Chekhov, I always recalled that Sunday afternoon of long ago, and with it the desire to create the impression that the atmosphere of an orchard as well as its shimmer of warm air were actually present on stage.

Even as a boy I liked to wander along deep paths in the paths and animal burrows. Perhaps it was this curiosity that later kept urging me to think about a plan for suspended walkways in the crowns of trees.

In the plains around Čáslav I loved the dominating presence of the city tower, the meadows and dales, the roads bordered by plum trees, pheasant yards, stone quarries, and sand pits. Once in Týn nad Vltavou at the top of a hill I discovered a very small country graveyard bordered by a white wall and wonderfully set in the surrounding countryside. In other words, I was fascinated by any defined space, its beautiful sensuousness.

And then I came to the realization that space could be

captured on drawing paper; not only the space that I could see but also space that I imagined. And the hardest lesson of all: it's possible to calculate how to make a bridge that won't collapse, but it's impossible to calculate how to make a thing beautiful.

Once in Čáslav I observed workers as they were preparing trenches in the square for the laying of cables. To this day I can see the care with which they removed the mosaic surface, systematically putting aside the stone cubes so that they could be readily replaced and still allow people to stroll by. I had always been convinced that the making of a proper table or chair was creative work, but here, in the square in Čáslav, I realized that any work can be creative, in direct proportion to the influence a person has on its rhythm and result.

This appreciation only strengthened itself as I first approached theatre and realized the sheer number of people required for the curtain to rise and the performance to begin each day at the same hour. A theatre company always reminds me of the crew of a ship. On a ship, everyone, from those who tend the boilers below decks, to ordinary seamen, officers, and up to the captain, has his own role which at any given moment only he can perform. Each role is equally important, and all of them together enable the captain to guide the ship safely from port to port.

It's the same in a good theatre. Each member values the work of his colleagues, because the work of each—intellectual or manual—is indispensable to the success of the whole performance. Theatre crafts, if they are truly to fulfill their function, demand individuality. Indeed, I'm convinced that the theatre will remain—and rightfully remain—the last organized activity of our time requiring skilled, hands-on labor.

It's said that every artistic work is a mirror of the artist's personality. I believe the same principle applies to every work that a person does gladly, with love, joy, and responsibility; a little bit of him remains in everything he does. Of course, we are all replaceable; but it's also true that an entire, unrepeatable world dies with each person. The more personally one marks what one does, the more one breathes one's own soul into it, the more evident is the imprint—and the sense of emptiness that remains after he or she is gone.

My oldest memories are of my father's furniture-making workshop in Čáslav. For a long time it was the only world that interested me. There for the first time I saw how raw material is transformed into an object. Scraps and wood shavings were things to play with; tools, machines, and motors were the first things I admired. My favorite toys came from there, all the dearer because I was present at their origin and understood them. As soon as I could borrow the simplest tools, I began to make my own toys. I didn't want store bought models, at least not until my uncle from Prague sent us—my two-year younger brother and me—a puppet theatre. That, of course, was a very special event.

I filled the laundry room with small chairs made by our apprentices as a test of their progress (putting together one of these small chairs was also one of my first ambitions). My first audience members were children from our street. I

handled the marionettes and did all the voices. But soon I had to admit that my miracle was obviously imperfect. I had to agree with the spectators, who were much more impressed by the puppet theatre in town, where the puppet handler couldn't be seen.

Soon after having devised—and built—my first *enclosed* theatre space to remedy the shortcomings of the unadorned laundry room, I realized again how much strain, effort, patience, and defeat every true search costs. But finally my theatre was born—a stage with a proper proscenium arch, a masked and spacious backstage area, and, of course, puppets. I usually didn't costume the puppets because what attracted me to them most was the play of their movements. This was my first intimate encounter with theatre. I couldn't have said what excited me most: the magical space that I detached from the rest of the world? The fairy-tale texts in which good always won out after many crises and hardships? Playing with light?

Light always attracted me. First I tried to discover how it originated and where it came from; only then did I begin to realize its miraculous effects. With heartfelt envy and wonder I watched the light in a stormy sky; the best I could do in my theatre was to rub together two carbon rods that had been plugged into the electric circuit. Later, I became fascinated by the light coming through a window curtain; the beam of light cast through a partially opened door into the darkness; the oblong pattern of light from windows; and I walked behind the lamplighter along darkened streets as he lit the gas lamps with a long pole. In other words, I was becoming aware of the inexhaustible power of light. And one day, much, much later, as I gazed spellbound at the way light streams through a gothic window, I conceived of the principle of theatrical contralight.[1]

My father's workshop produced furniture of every type, from the plainest to fashionable models (even according to Viennese catalogues). When it received an order to reconstruct the furniture in Phillip Castle near Čáslav, I first saw an interior with a distinctive period style. It made a great impression on me, even though it wasn't anything extraordinary. But whenever I have to create a period style interior on stage, that childish perception of complete harmony echoes within me.

During the economic crisis of the 1930s, my father even made windows, doors, wooden stairs, and wooden paneling. He also went around making official measurements of houses under construction; I began to be tantalized by the secret of how a house is built. From my experience in planning my puppet theatre, I already knew that a drawing is the beginning of everything. The workers in my father's workshop routinely drew individual details of their projects. I considered it self-evident that the basis of everything that's built or assembled is a well thought out and precisely drawn plan. But with a house it was more complicated. I toiled at copying plans of buildings that father was working on until I was weary, and it took a long time until I had a grip on the essentials. Then I started to work on a plan of a model town, with a house for each one in the family. I never had the opportunity to build such a town, only the plans and drawings of its individual parts that I developed with my students in the School of Applied and Industrial Arts. I've never even built a house. I live in a prefab, but I've improved the surroundings and I'm very happy to be at home.

I have drawn everything that I saw around me for as long as I can remember. Birds attracted me the most, and among birds, God knows why, storks. Then I started to copy pictures from magazines and books, until I copied all the drawings of Aleš that I could get my hands on. This youthful, childish passion has paid off many times when an immediate, technical adjustment was necessary and a draftsman was not to be found. Soon I began to make drawings of my own, leading to my determination to become a painter.

My father was not only an excellent craftsman but a distinctive personality with a vital interest in public affairs. The economic crisis of the 1930s inevitably affected him. As a twelve- or thirteen-year-old I had the opportunity to listen to the debates he occasionally had with a painter from whom our family had bought a few canvases. A former worker in a bankrupt lumberyard, he was a well-known speaker on the Communist platform on the first of May and before elections. It was in his disputes with father that I first heard arguments and judgments from another point of view, and the experience understandably attracted me, even without my understanding why. I often remembered that man, and I often yearned for everything to be as simple and clear as I thought it was then.

I was a small town boy; after crossing a few Čáslav streets I was in the countryside. Nature was an obvious place to play, not a special precinct to investigate. Only with scouting did I learn to understand it. Now when I go out for a walk early in the morning with our Alsatian, Pako, no matter what the weather, and there's not a soul around, I feel on the same good terms with nature as I did when I became an Eagle scout and prepared for still other scouting tests.

In the first years of secondary school I was most interested in geometry, drawing, and physics along with chemistry because of the exciting experiments involved. I had no idea that one day I'd find myself ignorant of the basic connections between physics and mathematics and would have to scramble to catch up. The subject in which I worked hardest, however, was Latin. I was in love up to my ears with our Latin teacher, which accounts for my remembering the foundations of Latin grammar to this day.

When I finished my basic academic courses in 1935, I got into an irreconcilable conflict with my father. He wanted me to continue my academic studies, while I persisted in my ambition to be a painter. I wanted to go to art school, but father didn't relent. In defiance I set about learning to be a carpenter in his workshop. Our mutual stubbornness did not make my apprenticeship a sweet experience. I wasn't spared a single apprentice assignment, from starting the heating in the morning to cleaning up at night. With clenched teeth, in full view of the whole town, I delivered finished orders on a handcart and went to special classes in carpentry theory. The stalemate went unbroken.

Of course, the further I got into the craft work itself, the more I enjoyed it, but I also painted and read as if obsessed. On the whole, these three years of defiant learning had a priceless significance for me. Working with a master craftsman, my father, I acquired the essence of a basic craft and learned to think in terms of its systematic order. My painting, thanks to my new grasp of one discipline, began to acquire a more thought-through appearance. I also began to read the basic canon of world literature. After receiving my apprentice and my journeyman papers three years later, I entered a two year master's school of carpentry in the Žižkov district of Prague. My powers of resistance were to be tested again.

And so, at eighteen, in the fall of 1938, forever to be associated with the Munich capitulation, I became

Svoboda and Václav Kašlik, Svoboda's most frequent director, in Montreal in 1985 during final rehearsals for Stauss's Salomé.

acquainted with our capital. Along with a large part of my generation, I found myself experiencing harshly contradictory realities. For those who survived, this clash determined the subsequent course of their lives; they'll carry it with them to the end of their days. Its essence was the feeling of a paralyzing impotence as we came face to face with a world which dealt with us as if we were worthless, dispensable entities. We fought against this feeling with feverish, often self-destructive activity that was goaded precisely by this frustrating impotence, and sustained by a grand and oversimplified dream of achieving a future harmony between humanity and the world.

I had always longed for Prague and, once there, couldn't get my fill of everything it offered me: unique architecture, galleries, bookstores, libraries, and theatres. But it was also the time of Munich, the Second Republic, the fifteenth of March and seventeenth of November 1939.[2] How to make sense of it all? With genuine gratitude I remember

An early Svoboda drawing for the 1943 Prague production of Hölderlin's Empedocles.

An early Svoboda drawing for the 1943 Prague production of Strindberg's The Crown Bride.

Mr. Vodák, my teacher at the Čáslav elementary and vocational school, a surprisingly well-rounded person and father's friend, who helped me to understand the time—and myself—during my weekly visits home. In 1942 he died in a concentration camp.

After two years at the master's school I moved on to a special school of interior architecture. All branches of the Žižkov school complex at that time had exceptionally fine teachers, including several professors from universities who came here after all Czech schools of higher education had been closed by the protectorate regime in 1939. Here I had the opportunity to listen to well known architects, and heard for the first time expert commentary on spatial composition. That the subject was taught by Professor František Tröster, I regard as one of the most fortunate accidents of my school years. Everything I've learned about spatial composition I learned from him. The Žižkov school curriculum included broader cultural subjects as well. An excellent philologist, for example, guided us not only through Czech but also through world literature. After graduating in 1943, I started to teach at the Žižkov school the following fall and continued there until the end of the war. I would spend a total of seven years there, from the age of eighteen to twenty-five. They were, of course, decisive years for us all.

The intensifying war and the Nazi terror forced my generation to mature quickly. We were thrust into situations that would mark us forever. The penetrating, painful awareness of the absolute dependence of one's fate on the particular form of a society or world to which it is subject is one of life's most enduring revelations. How was one to live in this cage? More than a few decided to resist the prevailing force and thereby experienced their fill of suffering and often even death. And more than a few were compelled to such suffering and death by chance, by the sheer blind will of force. We who stayed out of its direct reach lived from day to day, but we subordinated everything that we did to a vision…a magical incantation of the future. We drowned out our sense of impotence by intensive preparations for that future, hoping that perhaps we'd live to experience it. And none of us who gathered in the Karnet home doubted that art would play an extraordinary role in the postwar society as we conceived it. They included Václav Kašlík and Alfred Radok, artists with whom I was to work on major productions for many years.

I went to theatre almost daily in Prague. And completely by chance, during a medical visit in Čáslav, I actually made the acquaintance of Jindřich Honzl, who was already a classic figure in Czech theatre, and with whom I was to work after the war. I had already prepared a set in the Dušík theatre in Čáslav in 1942, for a presentation of *The Story of the Sun, the Moon, and the Windmill*, a tale by Božena Němcová, for the eightieth anniversary of her death, and for J. K. Tyl's *Marianka, Mother of the Regiment*, with which the Čáslav amateur group participated in a competition of Tyl plays held that year in Kutná Hora.

Once as I was helping an architect with some drawing in his studio, I came across a box full of Soviet theatre periodicals from the '20s and '30s, especially *Teatr i dramaturgija* and *Kamerny teatr*. I already knew the names of famous scenographers like Vasiljev, Rindin, Tatlin, Goncharova, Eksterova, and the names of directors like Tairov, Meyerhold, Stanislavski, and Okhlopkov. But here were photographs of productions, analyses of directors, critiques. Never have I put as much effort into learning a foreign language as I did then, just so that I could read all that material as soon as possible.

On September 8, 1943, our Prague group presented itself in the Smetana Museum under the name of The New Ensemble, and for the centennial of the poet Hölderlin's death staged dramatic fragments of his *Empedocles*.

Our second premiere in 1943 was Strindberg's *Crown Bride*. I made the set from two sets of stairs in the form of a hip roof, the top of which also provided an acting area 60 centimeters wide, running the length of the roof. Because the stairs had no risers, you could see right through them, transforming a hip roof of lathing into a stairway. A low platform with a ramp leading to it, which was the basic acting surface, was incorporated into the front staircase. Even in those early efforts I tried to encode all necessary functions and meanings into a single construction, to create an artifact that became an environment only as a result of the dramatic action. What seemed at first an abstract space became transformed through the play of the actors into a building, into a path to a lake, into a lake itself. It was, by the way, the first time I used a staircase as a dramatic element.

Scenography based on lighting is something I first tried seriously in 1944 for the production of Jiří Karnet's *Astray*. I based the entire scenography on seven hyperboloids of scrim material that were able to carry light along their surface. The scrim made the construction of the hyperboloids easier and also served as the basic background of the scene. The scenography—for which I had a detailed scenario—evoked the impression of a subterranean cave (for us it was the environment of the Nazi protectorate). Necessary changes were made solely by means of lighting and film and slide projection, with the awareness that the actors on the stage and on film had to be the same. Needless to say, I also drew from everything that E.F. Burian had tried before me.

Indeed, this production forced me to become more knowledgeable about the relationship of mathematics and physics, and taught me never to forget that any sort of searching, any sort of breakthrough or even improvisation must be based on a thorough knowledge of the essential characteristics or principles inherent in a given space and in the materials to be used within it.

Viewed in retrospect, the impotent feelings of despair and fear of my Žižkov years recede and, as in every recollection, the intense experience of human solidarity seems stronger. I lived through the Prague uprising of May 1945 with everyone else, and did what had to be done.[3] In the fall I was admitted to the School of Applied and Industrial Arts, with a major in Architecture. At the same time I also enrolled as a special student in the Philosophic Faculty, in the fields of art history and philosophy. To accomplish my goals—as I was told during that radio lecture—I had to try to learn and know everything.

THE THEATRE OF THE 5TH OF MAY

ife, it seems to me, has always raced by, but when I look at my grandson and granddaughter it seems that I must have sprinted through the last twenty years; on the other hand, I recall vividly not only months but often even days from forty or more years ago.

The war at long last was over, and with liberty came the first disappointment. Why does reality inevitably diverge so much from our visions? We had held large, institutional or "stone" theatres in contempt, and dreamed of small, experimental stages. All of us. But the longed-for liberation had barely passed before everyone dispersed; unexpected possibilities tempted some away from theatre—and some even into the scorned "stone" theatres. I felt betrayed by my friends. I decided to retreat into a full-time study of architecture at the School of Applied and Industrial Arts.

I was convinced and remain convinced that the best preparation for a scenographer is the study of architecture. An architect has to know how to comprehend and feel space, and he has to know how to master construction techniques. In fact, our best scenographers—with some honorable exceptions—have been architects. A school that educates scenographers directly—with no other solid discipline as its base—necessarily devotes itself to material that ought to form the content of subsequent, advanced study.

Scenography is not a scientific discipline; nor is dramaturgy. A person becomes a scenographer or a dramaturg through mastery of some fundamental method, whether literary, musical, or design (painting, drawing, sculpture, architecture), and then expands on it and applies it. To become a scenographer or dramaturg after four years of study of either discipline per se is not possible. Although such study may be broadly based, of necessity it provides only a superficial preparation; it lacks a base of fundamental scientific methodology.

For example, during our second year at the school, we were already doing a final project that really belonged to a more advanced class: a modification of the Smetana Embankment from the National Theatre to the Smetana footbridge. In my approach I addressed two basic issues: the reconstruction of older buildings, and the conceptual design of a certain limited space that contained the buildings.

I had to acknowledge that this section of the embankment provided the most complete and the most well-known view of Hradčany Castle, and yet I also had to take into consideration the opposite embankment with Střelecký Island. I made a pedestrian zone and park out of the area, and diverted motor traffic below the National Theatre, along Theatre Street and Karoliny Světlé Street. I earmarked the

Prokofiev. The Engagement in the Cloister. *Grand Opera of the Fifth of May, 1947. Dir: Václav Kašlík.*

historically significant buildings, recommended their restoration, razed other structures, and only added construction when it was essential to enclosing the given space. It was precisely with such demanding projects that I developed my own fundamental method, which I applied to my subsequent scenographic work. That's why I repeat that the specialized education of scenographers, only as scenographers, is inadequate if not impossible.

My exclusive commitment to rigorous academic exercises lasted exactly half a year. When Václav Kăslík, at that time the chief of opera in the Theatre of the Fifth of May (it was divided into the Great Opera and the Drama sections), invited me to work on Otakar Ostrčil's *Kunala's Eyes* in the late fall of 1945, I didn't—understandably enough—resist. Perhaps, indeed, because I naturally had never done any opera before in my life.

I stood spellbound before the limitless darkness of the huge stage, anxious whether the unfamiliar space would welcome me and open itself to me. I experience this sensation every time I meet a new environment, and I always wait in suspense—will it speak to me? This production with director Jiří Fiedler was the real beginning of my theatre career. The forgotten Ostrčil opera was based on a fairy tale libretto about Kunala, whose young stepmother had his eyes put out during his father's absence, and who, when his father gave her to him for punishment, forgave her. Ostrčil's opera became my first opportunity for the kind of scenography which—with great simplicity and yet directness—entered into the whole work as a further dramatic element.

The scenography was based on a stepped pagoda with two entrances above each other. In the first act it represented a palace with an extensive three-sided staircase—the embodiment of an unchanging, time-tested order. In the second act—as a reaction to a crime against this humane order, the blinding of Kunala—I laid the pagoda on its back, with its base upstage, so that the side staircases became vertical articulations of the architecture, with the acting surface restricted to the front part of the pagoda with the two entrances in a reversed position. In the third act, the pagoda was set on its pointed end, as if a mirage had suddenly appeared above the floor. Kunala now had no eyes, but he could see better than those who did. The quick transformations of the pagoda were made possible by using a structural cube as a core to which component surfaces were attached in various configurations. Soon afterward, on this same large stage, Alfred Radok and I began our long-lasting work together. Lord, what joy we experienced working on *The Tales of Hoffmann* in 1946! We spoke the same language and delighted in the same things. Everything seemed possible, as if we were both intoxicated. The text

and music lent themselves to our ideas and immediately prompted others.

The magician D'Appertuto drove up in a Tatra auto to a power line tower, whose insulators flashed electric charges; the youthful Hoffmann made his way to Olympia (enclosed in a huge crystal ball) on a path full of shrubs with tiny

Ostrčil. Kunala's Eyes. *Grand Opera of the Fifth of the May, Prague, 1945. Dir: J. Fiedler.*

white spheres. In addition to lighting towers and bridges and gridiron flooring, a little antique theatre, including a sculpture of a lion, hung from a block and tackle; in Giuletta's scene, we conjured up Venice with painted flats.

On the main part of the stage, a ballet was danced among candlesticks arranged around the floor. Along with a large multipurpose skeletal frame with lights and a platform with a small stage, a large sphere was the only stage prop. It opened in the third act like a locket: in one half was Antonia's small room, in the other a photograph of her mother. We created a sense of timelessness by placing signs of various epochs next to each other. The collage literally swelled with poetic imagination, colors, sounds, and forms, and yet was stylistically coherent.

We also realized that works by Offenbach, Gounod, Donizetti, and others like them—in order to speak to today's world—can neither be parodied nor reproduced in their original form. But if we used realistic elements that reminded us of the original time, and estranged them and put them into new relationships, a new and effective theatrical reality resulted. Then we could provide Marguerite in *Faust* with a sewing machine rather than a spinning wheel, transform Walpurgisnacht into a night in Paris, and thereby only strengthen the impact of the music and theme.

Soon after the premiere of *The Tales of Hoffmann* I was summoned by the director of the entire Theatre of the Fifth of May, composer Alois Hába. He and Václav Kašlík proposed that I become the production chief of this huge theatre. So much for my decision to be nothing but a full-time student!

My life is poor in incidents and events that don't involve work. That's simply the way it's been, and I have no regrets. One evening, after I had already been at the National Theatre for many years, the head of opera, Hanuš Thein, hurried to our home. He began to explain his idea of the production on which we were both to work. In the middle of his comments he suddenly stopped and said, "I'm going home, chief. When you get rid of that blank stare and are ready to listen to me, let me know." He was right. I had no idea what he was saying, because I was thinking of something completely different, of the work in which I was buried up to my ears. I can't tear myself away under those circumstances, and I exasperate people around me because of it, but I can't help it.

But let me return to 1946, that year that was so memorable for me. I was in the second year of the School of Applied and Industrial Arts, and I had behind me my baptism as a designer in professional theatre. Now on top of it I was to become chief of stage and workshop operations. At the same time I had only the slightest experience with the operations or organization of the theatre.

The Theatre of the Fifth of May (now the Smetana Theatre) had formerly been the German opera house, and Czechs had worked in its shops from the beginning; understandably, they remained after the war. What saved me in that crucial adventure was my lucky convergence with genuine experts in their craft. I was a certified master carpenter, a student of architecture, and a fledgling designer; facing me were people who were masters of theatre in their respective professions.

At first, I felt naked amid thorns. I would have given

Offenbach. The Tales of Hoffmann. *Grand Opera of the Fifth of May, Prague, 1946. Dir: Alfred Radok.*

Dvořák. Rusalka. *National Theatre, Prague, 1991. Dir: Nikolaus Windisch-Spoerk.*

Offenbach. Tales of Hoffmann. *State Theatre, Ostrava, 1947. Dir: Bohumil Hrdlička.*

anything to know what they knew. I had nothing to give. I carefully edged forward, by instinct, while feeling their half ironic, half curious glances on me: "Well then, son, how are you going to handle *that* problem?" I can't recall ever experiencing greater anxiety than in front of those dyed-in-the-wool theatre workers. I was in the theatre from morning till night, tapping their knowledge like the hungriest apprentice.

The Theatre of the Fifth of May was run by trade unions, and as things developed after the war this led to its having exceptionally young artistic ensembles and very experienced technical personnel. It was literally a workshop. To this day, no matter where I may be, I long for it—so much was not only possible but taken for granted forty years ago! We issued no manifestos, and yet we handled every work as if it were a newly discovered gem that needed cleaning in order to shine again. The entire theatre felt as if each premiere were an original creation, their very own, no matter which of us was doing it. We lived for theatre; the workshops operated day and night before a premiere and then had perhaps a week off.

Preparation time was thereby essentially shortened, and a creative tension was sustained until the premiere. Costumes, for example, were sewn only after the actors had worked into their roles and it was possible to make meaningful decisions. We hunted for materials wherever we could. Our buyer drove all over the republic collecting specimens on his motorcycle! And the entire operation, whose one goal was a successful production, was unbelievably inexpensive in comparison to today's operations. And why not! After all, there were no superfluous people in it. The collective wouldn't have put up with them.

More than any other experience, my years in the Theatre of the Fifth of May enabled me to understand what theatre really means and, mainly, what it might become. Theatre can never be anything other than a constantly evolving creative workshop, in which everyone is totally committed to the same goal.

Before the end of 1946 Kašlík and I presented Smetana's *The Bartered Bride*. And we created a scandal. My scenography employed a blue cyclorama in front of which shone a sun made of thin wood strips resembling those at the bottom of a potato basket. The only solid element of the cottages on the green were their gable facades; the walls were of white cloth with perforated embroidery windows; below were pleated curtains instead of a foundation. Above all this hung three straw figures decorated with meadow flowers, a white silhouette of the village, and colored ribbons and bows. The entire stage was wrapped within a horseshoe formed by low, three-dimensional roofs of cottages, which looked as if they bordered a deeply carved road. That was the environment for Kecal's entrance in the second act and for his hurdle run over the roofs.

In the first act the entirely three-dimensional roof of the tavern was hung from ribbons; the tavern also had walls of cloth on two sides. During the "Alas, alas, the end of joy, worries are a-coming" number, the drinking farmers could defend themselves against the crowd of infuriated women by turning the tavern so that the women faced a wall.

Large blossoms of suspended sunflowers created an

instantly intimate setting for Marie's and Jeník's "faithful love." During Marie's aria in the second act, "I know a girl, burning with love for you," Marie rocked Vašek on the little roof of one of the cottages. Say what you will, it was absolutely right for Smetana. His music sparkled with life and movement, and so did the stage.

But it created a scandal. Our irreverent, cheery production upset critics accustomed to the sentimental, folklorist approach that had become a tradition on our stage. Scandals have always been part of art and there's no reason why they shouldn't be. On the contrary, artistic progress relies on the defiance of conventions, and conventions naturally resist. I'll never understand why it's necessary to suppress this natural process.

K. H. Mácha provoked scandals, K. J. Erben was immediately put into school textbooks, and they both became canons of Czech poetry. Alban Berg's *Wozzek* gave Prague's mayor a stroke, but not even this drastic event diminished the lasting significance of Berg's creation. And what if there's been a mistake? Mistakes, if they are large-scale, creative mistakes, may prove more valuable than a sure success. Is there any danger that everyone will immediately start imitating mistakes? The anxiety to avoid scandals only leads to temerity on all levels, beginning with the choice and treatment of scripts and ending with the production itself.

Another scandal erupted around our production of *The Magic Flute* with director Bohumil Hrdlička in 1957. What in fact had we done? We rejected the historical fairy tale version. In order to reveal the extraordinary multitude of emotive and ideational associations within the work, we approached it as a timeless fantasy. In an abstract space shaped by lighting, we dressed the performers in contemporary social attire. Did it harm Mozart? Certainly

Smetana. The Bartered Bride. *Grand Opera of the Fifth of May, Prague, 1946. Dir: Václav Kašlík.*

43

not. Did it prevent the singers from singing well? Again, no. It was only that the significance of Shikaneder's tale touched the present and perhaps hinted at something relevant and problematic to some in the audience. There was no danger of massive degeneration in the production of Mozart's operas, and no one followed in our footsteps.

When I repeated *The Magic Flute* four years later, this time with director Kašlík, we based it on a completely different principle, but still centered in lighting. The stage was full of triangular mirrors made of plexiglass. The mirrors reflected period painted flats placed offstage at the sides, where they couldn't otherwise be seen—the realm of the Queen of Night, the realm of Sarastro, and the world of Papageno. In both productions we staged *The Magic Flute* with contemporary means simply as a fable, but we revealed to the spectator another possible view of Mozart's masterful work.

The furor around *The Bartered Bride* in 1946 was more understandable in that it belongs among works whose stagings have become so encrusted with tradition that their original sense and impact are no longer evident and palpable.

Despite all the enthusiasm about Smetana, he remains undiscovered by us to this day. We simply regard him as the Alois Jirásek of music, and that's the way we stage his operas. I can't help my view that Kašlík's staging remains the optimal one. It made the stage dance, responded to every change in the dramatic situation, and precisely intuited the right degree of hyperbole and naturalism for the work. Just to recall the start of Kašlík's second act in the tavern! It communicated the feeling of life's fullness, love, passion, sorrow and humor, as it really must be felt in *The Bartered Bride*. This unusual, contemporary, and intelligible approach allowed spectators to see the work for the first time.

When we did *The Bartered Bride* with Kašlík at the National Theatre in 1955, it was called the "kerchief *Bride*." The space was defined by a curtain of large kerchief-like drapes, which made it possible to move freely from one situation to another. I've done *The Bartered Bride* with other directors in other countries. The closest to my original concept was the 1978 production with John Dexter at the Metropolitan Opera in New York. But never again was it as brimming with life, Smetanavian, and yet contemporary as it was with Kašlík in 1946. Our notorious production resonates with energy in my memory, while Bartered Brides

dressed like Czardasz princesses trot around the world—leaving everyone tranquilized.

Václav Kašlík is an unrecognized and underestimated prophet of modern opera staging.[1] Another of our important Smetana productions was *Dalibor* in the National Theatre in 1961. It was the period after the Brussels Expo of 1958, and the workshops of the National Theatre were operating at an improved level. We wanted to test our strength and resources, balancing creative potentials against economic costs. The premise of our work on *Dalibor* was that movement and rhythm, and movement and music, must

Mozart. The Magic Flute. *National Theatre, Prague, 1957. Dir: B. Hrdlička. The addition of a ceiling piece adds another dimension. Some of the mirrored surfaces reflect the rococo embellishments of the eighteenth-century theatre auditorium. itself.*

work in absolute harmony. To achieve this end, I would have to abandon my previous methods.

Slide and film projection technology required rapid changes of groundplan. Lighting can change a space in a

44

fraction of a second, whereas tangible scenography is slower and, worse, it's noisy. Nevertheless, the stage action demanded that we integrate the transformations in the groundplan with changes in lighting.

Our first attempts of this nature were at the Laterna Magika (1958), followed by the 1959 production of *Hamlet* at the National Theatre. In *Hamlet* I also used contralights as a primary expressive force for the first time. In *Dalibor* I had two massive prisms on stage, eccentrically placed on two turntables. One flat panel suspended from the flies also served as a projection surface. The eccentric placement of the prisms on respective turntables enabled their independent, fluid spatial changes. Together with the contralights—three curtains of light, each ten meters wide that shone at a thirty degree angle toward the audience—the prisms gave the impression that their movements were not those of a carousel, but those of scenography moving toward the audience or away from it. All the changes were precisely integrated with the actions of the performers and with the music. The movement of the scenography became a legitimate, proven expressive element, which in the professional literature acquired the designation "kinetic staging." In later years I developed and enriched this principle further.

An example of another type of staging based on lighting was our production of Dvořák's *Rusalka* at the National in 1960, which has remained in the repertoire ever since.[2]

Kašlik's unconventional and creative approach was first revealed in Janáček's *Káta Kabanová*. Each encounter with Janáček is a revelation for me; I never tire of him. It never ceases to amaze me that while the whole world is enchanted by him, we at home barely keep him in the repertoire. The fact that he was his own librettist makes his librettos that much more significant in his work. In Janáček, as distinct from other composers, the spectator wants to and must understand the text, because it is essential in conveying the meaning of the whole work.

Janáček is extraordinarily difficult and extraordinarily

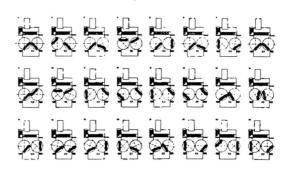

attractive for a scenographer. His visions of the stage are so precise and meaningful that it's impossible to change them. We may only try to penetrate more deeply to their very root, to make them more distinct on the stage—the most difficult challenge of all! Take his description of the chamber in which Káta and Varva sit at a window. Her husband's away and Káta laments, "Why don't people fly like birds...fly?" How to capture the concrete atmosphere as well as Káta's state of mind? It's all there in the music. A scenographer must either retreat completely into the background or else put himself on the line and find something to add.

For Kašlík's *Káta Kabanová* in the Theatre of the Fifth of May in 1947, I chose a tree as the basis of the scenography. I returned to the opera again many times, but

Janáček. Káta Kabanova. *Grand Opera of the Fifth of May, Prague, 1947. Dir: Václav Kašlík.*

never with that same boldness. It was truly a liberated set.

This was the kind of apple tree that I saw around me as a child in the country. At times their branches almost crawled along the ground; orchard keepers supported them with heavy wooden poles, often anchoring their trunks in cement. Such an apple tree, now larger than life, became my dramatic space. Its thick branches served as paths; the weaker ones, aiming upward, delimited the acting area and were its idealized exterior. A commanding presence, it dominated the space above a stage floor covered by a watertight carpet whose crumpled surface simulated puddles and mud. Freely laid planks served as wooden footways.

The whole tree was supported by both wooden and mortar pillars in the form of Russian folk architecture of the seventeenth century; these pillars also helped to create the interiors. The steel construction of the apple tree was masked by a covering made of short wooden slivers and strips resembling the bark of an old tree trunk. I supplemented the various scenes with furniture, properties, street lamps, wooden fences, or sculpted crows in flight, and I hung icons on the trunk of the tree. The entire construction stood on a turntable within a curved white cyclorama. It disappeared with the vertical unfurling of an inner black cyclorama, and a countermovement of the turntable created a new, black space. We worked without any projections at all. The lighting units were placed in such a way as to cast onto the cyclorama shadows of the decor, of the properties, and even of the actors, often during the movement of the turntable and the performers' actions. By means of lighting, things freed themselves of their everyday appearance and were justified solely by the genre and style of the play. The wooden tree played the role of nature as a

consoling force as well as an impenetrable prison.

For a production of Verdi's *Aida* in 1947, again with Kašlík, I used the principle of stairs for a second time. Stairs, in the most varied forms, fascinated me for years. We also tackled Prokofiev's *Engagement in the Cloister*, still in 1947, with emphasis on its comic element. The main scenographic elements of this production were transformations; trees became Pierrots from the commedia dell'arte, doors changed into keyholes, and so on. The scenography itself was created by eight wagons that shifted around on a curtainless stage during the play; individual pieces of the structures were ready to respond and adjust to the variously positioned sources of light.

Much later I worked with Kašlík on Tchaikovsky's *The Queen of Spades*, first in Ottawa in 1976 and then in Houston. To begin with, Kašlík's dramaturgical adaptation, a very felicitous rendering entirely in keeping with the music, was rooted in the premise that the entire story occurs in Herman's mind during his confinement in a mental asylum. The real world of the asylum cell and the world of fantasy never meet; they're divided not only by visible means such as transparent walls, but also by the ever-present inner tension which changes every longing into frustrated despair.

Changes of scene occurred by means of a platform that moved silently on a cushion of air; it measured 30 x 6 meters and was a meter high. It resembled a skiff on water, handled by two people. Hallucinations slowly suppressed reality entirely, until finally the line between reality and hallucination disappeared. The doors opened and stayed open and would never close again. Behind them was nothingness, death.

In 1947, in addition to *Káta Kabanová*, *Aida*, and

Engagement in the Cloister, I also prepared *Tosca* and *Rigoletto* for the Theatre of the Fifth of May. *Tosca* came into the repertoire as a replacement for a production I no longer recall. One evening, director Karel Jernek came to see me in my "atelier"—a cramped space some four by two and a half meters—and informed me that he had to start blocking the day after tomorrow. My work would need to be done overnight!

In terms of the geometrical perspective of the dramatic space, I chose the point of view of a frog and a bird, and then proceeded as a baroque architect would have done. For the cathedral interior, I leaned the entire scenography at a forty-five degree angle diagonally to the left starting from

impossible assignment was finished in time.

Catastrophe intervened at the technical rehearsal. The time limit for each scene change was exceeded by so much that the rhythm of the performance would have been completely thrown off. I had underestimated certain critical laws of set construction in relation to scene changes. The whole theatre lived through this catastrophe with us and kept faith that we'd find a way out. Finally we found an answer. By hanging most of the scenery from the flies, we cut the changes down to twenty minutes. But I emerged with the principle engraved in my memory that even the very best plans are worthless unless they can be integrated within standard theatre practices.

Not long afterward, in 1948, we experienced another shock. I had prepared scenography for a production of *La Boheme* at Ústí nad Labem with precise plans, models, three-dimensional pieces, and notes. On the day of the technical rehearsal I set out early in the morning by auto with my wife, Libuše. By eight in the morning we got in the back door and went up to the balcony of the theatre, where no one else had yet appeared. I was surprised that scenery for some other production still stood on the stage; they hadn't yet changed sets, which meant that we had at least two hours of free time. We went out for some tripe soup and returned at ten. Although there was a lot of activity in the theatre, the same set still stood on the stage. It turned out to be my own set that I hadn't recognized at all! Of course, I hurriedly tried to correct what could be corrected. This thoroughly disagreeable experience made me appreciate all the more our workshops in Prague.

Rigoletto was another production I prepared with Radok (see photo page 37).

Verdi. *Tosca. Grand Opera of the Fifth of May, Prague, 1947. Dir. K. Jernek*

the footlights (the frog perspective). In Scarpia's salon I then leaned it from the top edge of the proscenium arch toward the rear of the stage (the bird perspective). For the scene at Castel Sant'Angelo, I again used the frog perspective, but this time diagonally to the right. The actors, therefore, never played in front of the scenography but inside its two-part construction.

The bottom part of the picture was built like an actual architectonic object, like a solid pedestal, which supported an extended illusionistic superstructure created by a painted perspective that ended as the cyclorama. The entire stage for *Tosca* was divided by an invisible horizontal line into an architectonic and a painted part. Optically, of course, both merged into one unit and were terminated by the imaginary "heaven" of a baroque cupola and a theatrical "heaven" in the scene on the ramparts of the Castel Sant'Angelo.

I was extremely proud of this overnight labor of mine. In the morning I called the workshop together and we began to make drawings on canvas right away. The master craftsmen immediately saw what I was after, and the work went ahead instinctively. The seemingly

The entire stage was based on the principle of a theatre inside a theatre. On a turntable some twelve meters in diameter I built a complete replica of a stage with its technical apparatus including backstage equipment—a wind machine, rotating ocean waves to be used for a storm, and so on—in the style of the Italian scenographer Galli Bibiena. Around this complete mini-theatre, which even had its period painted curtain and decor for each scene, I created a backstage area including dressing rooms for quick changes, a small salon where gentlemen waited for the friends in the ballet, even a booth for the stage manager—everything that makes the backstage a microcosm of the theatre.

We precisely maintained the structure of the individual acts of *Rigoletto* and the number of their scene changes. The spectator first saw a carefully blocked scene from its conventional perspective, and then, unexpectedly, from the backstage perspective. Actually, two lines of action progressed together in parallel. The first according to the libretto, and the second made possible, of course, by the music: stagehands religiously listening to the hero's aria, ballet dancers getting ready for their entrances, the attendant knitting, and suddenly next to her, his back to the audience, the commandant singing only to her. Thanks to the rotating stage, the spectators gradually perceived all this as one entity, dominated by music. The scenes were not changed during intermissions, after large units, but shifted during the entire flow of the opera, divided into a series of sequences, which made the changes part of the dramatic action, like the movement and actions of the performers.

In 1948 Radok and I tackled Leoncavallo's *Pagliacci*, which Radok conceived as pure commedia dell'arte. The entire performance echoed this concept with consistent and pure stylization. My setting consisted of a ramp covered with a harlequin cloak so as to suggest both a street and a modern highway. Onto this ramp rode a car—a prism made of cubes, with wheels from an old theatre cart.

The performance began and ended, as was Radok's custom, with a ritual. The car rode up, and on both sides of the ramp—a highway terminating in poplars—stood the chorus. Jutting above the car was a flat with a rosy window, the sole visible symbol of the commedia dell'arte, in front of which the entire action was played out. At the end, the chorus disassembled the entire scene except for the window and two downstage flats at each side of the proscenium, while the ballet entered and covered the entire stage with a funereal black cloak. Even in those early days, Radok's

explain it—maybe I should take off my clothes!" he lamented. "Try it," Hába laconically said. Radok instantly stripped, and lo and behold—the shock helped and everything turned out well.

We had two years of joyful toil behind us. We were proud of our theatre. It began to have its own distinctive signature, its style, and every new member contributed something to its identity. We had moved past the starting line in our work and also, for the most part, in life. (During those years I married and had a daughter, Šarka.[3]) We all had many plans, and we knew that work and more work with little money was waiting for us all. But it was only at odd free moments that we jokingly wondered if it might not perhaps be easier to rob a bank. In other words, our prevailing feeling was that nothing could stop us on our road to a liberated theatre.

The decision to dissolve the Theatre of the Fifth of May and merge it with the National Theatre under the name of the Smetana Theatre came like a bolt out of the blue. At first we thought it was a false alarm, that it simply couldn't be true. Could the stroke of a pen destroy the opportunity that May 1945 provided Prague—the possibility of finally having two opera stages with different approaches and aims? We couldn't grasp the decision, didn't understand it, rejected the practical considerations (there certainly weren't

Tchaikovsky. The Queen of Spades. National Arts Center, Ottawa, 1976. Dir: Václav Kašlik.

almost unbelievably precise blocking was evident.

During rehearsals for *Rigoletto* a scene occurred that became a staple of gossip in the theatre. The title role was sung by a Yugoslavian singer; he was accustomed to the traditional blocking of the opera and got into conflict with Radok. The dispute ultimately needed to be resolved by the director of the whole theatre, Hába, in the presence of the entire creative collective. Hába wanted each side to explain its position to the other and reach an agreement democratically. The discussion dragged on, with the director explaining his conception several times, but in vain. "My lord! how else can I

any artistic ones), but no one stood up for us, and we became painfully aware that something was ending that would never be repeated again.

To this day I remain convinced that it was a bad decision. The company that ensued never became a true company—there still are separate orchestras and choruses in the National and Smetana theatres—and neither of the two stages has its own distinctive features.[4] For a brief time we managed a certain autonomy, but around 1950 the full consolidation was completed. I shall never stop regretting it. And never again did I have a feeling of such tight, freely chosen kinship as in the Theatre of the Fifth of May.

Opposite: Sophocles. Oedipus the King. *National Theatre, Prague, 1963. Dir: Miroslav Macháček. The risers of the stairs were perforated by holes to enhance the acoustics of the live orchestra situated behind the stairs. Photo: Jaromír Svoboda*

THE NATIONAL
THEATRE

In his 1970s memoirs, the great actor Ladislav Pešek talks of his first encounter with the National Theatre: "As a boy I arrived for my first visit to Prague, with my parents, who were members of the Brno State Theatre. When we stood before the National Theatre, Dad took off his hat, and Mamma, who was moved, clasped her hands. This recollection from early childhood permanently engraved itself in my memory."

For my generation, the National Theatre signified history rather than the present, especially our present. And when, despite our resolve, we finally did join together after the war in one of the "stone" theatres, it was the Theatre of the Fifth of May which had a very contemporary and, like us, a very brief existence.

I came to know Jindřich Honzl better in 1946. He was now head of drama at the National Theatre, and I did the scenography for his production of Martens and Obey's *Wastrels in Paradise* in the Studio of the National Theatre. My setting was actually nothing more than furniture placed here and there in the Belgian countryside, furniture with precisely defined variable functions. The bed came apart to form a garden, as needed; the wardrobe became a helicopter, and pillows became flags. Barrels were transformed into hell; snowmen were inside with pots on their heads and carrots for noses.

One day later that year, Honzl called me into his office and after a brief conversation invited me to work with him on a production of the Čapek brothers' play, *The Insect Comedy*. I was startled first by the the prospect of working at the National Theatre; but more formidable was the challenge of that particular play. Why, the original production in the 1920s was still fresh in people's minds! Of course, I was attracted by Jindřich Honzl's unconventionality and his feeling for the inner complexities of creative imagination. But I still felt anxious and out of place. I walked around the National Theatre, simply not myself. I was also supposed to design the costumes, which would mean confronting celebrated actors whom I knew only from the audience.

My work with Jindřich Honzl turned out to be a textbook model of collaborative work. We agreed so deeply that I

Martens and Obey. Wastrels in Paradise. *National Theatre Studio, Prague, 1946. Dir: S.Vyskočil.*

scarcely made any changes to my original sketches. Our work was based on the contrast of the artificial with the real. We had cobwebs of antennas, insects with propellers (like airplanes) and flowers blossomed into ladies' art nouveau hats. Nature sprouted as a patch of grass enlarged to human scale and transformed into a caricature of the world, in which trees were replaced by factory chimneys and pipes, out of which thrust the tops of real trees where woodpeckers perched. The Ant World was a disk of Swiss cheese with openings leading to spiral passages; the Beetle

vision shaped by Čapek and Honzl, but by me as well.

Some twenty years later, in 1965, I did the same work completely differently, with Miroslav Macháček. Of course, even Macháček's very concept was entirely in keeping with the way this definitively social play modulates in meaning according to the social context of each production. Now the recognizable everyday human reality of the beginning and end of the play openly emphasized the relationship between contemporary man and society, as perceived by our audiences daily. The rest of the play—the extended

Photo inset: Jarka Burian

Čapek, K. and J. The Insect Comedy, National Theatre, Prague, 1946. Dir: J. Honzl.

Photo: Jaromír Svoboda

Čapek, K. and J. The Insect Comedy. *National Theatre, Prague, 1965. Dir: Miroslav Machacek.*

functioned like a bulldozer; other hard shelled insects pulled wagons filled with ore, and the Moths descended from the flies with little white parachutes and covered the stage. In the final Tramp scene, the chorus held real spruce branches in their hands.

The principal roles were played by established, seasoned actors. For the first time in my life, the fullness of my imagination was realized on stage. For the first time I understood what can be accomplished by great actors with minimal space and resources. I also realized that without such actors, all efforts are worthless. The production was a

metaphor of insect life—became a very relevant satire on our society at the time.

The staging employed simple and obvious resources, but they created a complex image that hit the audience all at once, in an instant—that was the essence of our concept. The artificial devices of the first production were exchanged for the concrete imagistic possibilities of concrete materials. A mirror is one of these, and the varieties of its transformations are infinite; it seems to me that I'm only beginning to grasp its capabilities. In *Hamlet* I added moveable panels to the mirror principle, and here in the

Čapek play a turntable with some ten layers of variously painted cloth coverings. The resulting images were unique and dramatically functional. The floor and its reflection in the mirrors became a surface on which it was possible to indicate fairly precisely the individual scene changes by revealing the sequential layers of cloth coverings. If the standard scenographic guide in the '20s was a painted rendering and in the '30s a three dimensional model, then in the '60s it was a groundplan, lighting scenario, and a filmed record of a kinetic model.

The chief problem of Macháček's production lay in determining the shape of the mirrors and the angle at which their surface ought to be suspended above the colorfully illuminated turntable in order to capture its image most

Gogol. Revizor. *National Theatre, Prague, 1948. Dir: Jindřich Honzl. "The backside of Czarist Russia."*

quickly. And yet it was also a miracle with its cards laid on the table: the viewer knew a mirror was involved, but was nonetheless amazed by its possibilities. The mirrors, in tandem with the rotating turntable, did not create a normal static image, but a dynamic image, abstract and yet accurate, of a swarming ant-hill that seemed to grow in full view of the spectators' eyes: an insect world covering the earth and sky, the entire cosmos.

And the starting point of it all was a hexagon, a mirror composed of hexagons like a honeycomb. Whenever I think of those two productions, so different and yet so Čapekesque, I realize that in the first one we knew that ants in nature recognize a surplus of either sex or any danger threatening them by scent, and the female ants determine the sex of their offspring accordingly. We wanted to make this canniness of nature resemble the world of man. In the second production, on the contrary—if we were to be true to our source, to ourselves, and to the spectator of the '60s— we had to turn humbly to nature as to the greatest miracle and search for traces of humanity within it, to reveal nature's laws and study them. And to create the setting for

this production, I had to grasp the principle of a honeycomb and the laws of light and reflection.

In 1948 Jindřich Honzl gave me two colossal tasks at once: Gogol's *Revizor* and the brothers Mrštík's *Maryša*. For *Revizor*, the director had a very simple request: "I want a scene that will show that Gogol gathered everything bad that he had ever seen in Russia and put it in this play." Well, he got it.

The set stood on a turntable. At first glance its construction culminated in proud towers of Russian churches and their magnificence. As soon as it turned, however, the spectator began to realize that he was actually seeing only fragments of buildings, with straw peeking out; in fact, pig-sties and goat-pens could be recognized behind the gilded surfaces: the facade and backside of Czarist Russia. A Potemkin village that shone like gold in front, but from behind—stage flats, and behind them boxes of refuse, piles of furniture, windows, doors and chandeliers, in short a pell-mell heap; and people crawled through all of this on several levels. They crowded into Khlestakov's room like bedbugs, they were everywhere; the characters took on the look of their environment and the environment adapted itself to them. The Inn was situated in the upper part of the scenography and was reached by stairs.

Whenever a visitor burst through the door, he dropped straight down a full meter. Sáša Rasilov, who played the Mayor, chased me around the theatre with a cane, shouting all the way to the dressing rooms that he wasn't going to have his legs broken because of some novice's bright ideas! He didn't break them and soon he took me back into his favor. The direction and the set fused and created an exceptional unity. Once again, the casting was perfect.

But with *Maryša* by the Mrštík brothers I was at a loss. How was I to get a grip on this most realistic of our realistic dramas? Other than during my youthful work in Čáslav, I had no experience with the Czech dramatic repertoire; it didn't attract me. Yet *Maryša* is incontestably a truthful and modern work, among the best plays in our language.

Honzl's admirable abilities of analysis and precise blocking rescued me again. The renderings, which I did in oil, shone with contrasting white and dark brown pigments. Built once again on a turntable, the set consisted of white walls and escutcheons. The only additions were furniture and props, but the whole had the effect of a real village. Honzl's untraditional approach included casting relatively young performers in the older roles. The basic human drama of the story now stood out all the more. Honzl's ability to maintain a precise relation between realism and stylization infused the play with an unusual appeal.

J. K. Tyl's *Hardheaded Woman* was an even more realistic production, in 1952. Appropriately enough for Tyl, everything was authentic and yet fairytale-like. Brilliant acting sparkled with wit but also touched young and old with its pure humanity.

A few years earlier, when Jindřich Honzl was head of drama production and František Götz the chief dramaturg, we had shifted over to the National Theatre. After the death of Václav Gottlieb, in 1950, I became chief of artistic-technical operations. I naturally wanted a theatre workshop like the one I had been used to, in which everyone was willing to do whatever was necessary to fulfill his

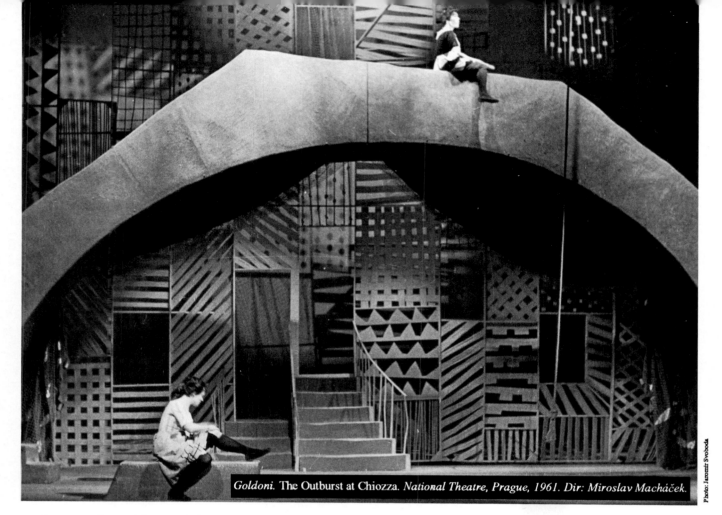

Goldoni. The Outburst at Chiozza. *National Theatre, Prague, 1961. Dir: Miroslav Macháček.*

assignment. Several key technical personnel such as the Frey brothers came with me from the Theatre of the Fifth of May. Jaroslav who was especially close to me, a former scenepainter and hand-letterer, in time became the head of construction and stage inspector. He never stopped speculating about how to make a thing better, and not once did he shy away from a formidable obstacle. Even his death was characteristic, while in the midst of his work on a tour of the National Theatre in Italy.

Jan Fremund also came. He, too, was originally a scenepainter, and then for years a model-maker. No matter how eccentric some proposals seemed at first glance, his clever hands readily embodied them in models. Also joining us was architect František Hořejš, my fellow pupil at the Žižkov school, who gave up an assured position for our cause. The crazy risks we took, secure in our faith that František would see us through! To this day I continue to rely on him.

What *didn't* these people know how to do? Václav Skokan and Jaroslav Kudrna were carpenters and true masters of their craft; Robert Klička, originally chief of the paintshop became head of document preparation for the scene shops. The master carpenter was able to step up to the drawing board and draw an alternative construction variant for a designer. The metal worker often came up with a much simpler and still functional version of what was originally designed. The painters demonstrated that their solution could in large part be better than what the model called for; and so on. Our unwritten principle was not to take on people based only on their formal qualifications. First we searched out those who really loved theatre, craftsmen who would proceed to make the individual disciplines their own. Many of the new recruits came from old theatre families in which craftsmanship was handed down from generation to generation.

Our chief hallmark was quality work done promptly, economically, and with progressive methods. As in the Theatre of the Fifth of May, all considerations were subordinated to preparations for an opening night. It was clear to us that a director is unable to judge his total concept until he sees it on stage. Only then does his final, distinctive creative work begin. He must have adequate time for that critical stage of his work, time to adjust his premises during rehearsals. It's simply not possible to calculate from a model just how the overall blocking will look on stage in the finished scenography. Who can know in advance how the actors will move in their costumes, and how they'll handle the props? And what if the director gets a

Svoboda and former colleague Jan Fremund at 1990 exhibit of Svoboda's work.

Hrubin. A Sunday in August. *National Theatre, Prague, 1958. Dir: Otomar Krejča.*

revolutionary, perhaps brilliant idea only at the moment when he sees everything come together? We didn't have a rehearsal room in which we could mount the scenography and have everyone adjust to it during the rehearsal period. And what's much worse, we still don't have it, not even today—after all our restructuring. Theatre is theatre when it can remain hospitable to constructive change up to the last moment. As distinct from film, theatre must allow itself this license if it is to remain a truly "lively" art.

The production capacity of the National Theatre workshops gradually exceeded normal needs by roughly ten percent. We were occasionally able to help the Vinohrady Theatre, The Theatre Behind the Gate, the S.K. Neumann Theatre, the ABC Theatre, and others. If necessary, we could turn out an entire set in a week, as happened, for example, with Goldoni's *The Outburst at Chiozza* (1961).

The National Theatre workshops' range of activities also gradually extended itself. The Scenographic Laboratory came into being, led by Miroslav Kouřil; eventually it outgrew the confines of the theatre and became independent. A new generation of photographers arrived with the tireless Miloš Wokoun and established a photo department as well as a slide department. A design archive and props repository was built up by Zdena Schmoranzová, and a special unit for costume production

by Jan Vitík. Květoslav Bubeník (former head of the paint shops and later designer for the National Theatre), Oldřich Šimáček, and costume designer Jindřiška Hirschová were the first designers to follow and maintain quality control of a production (whoever was specifically designing it) from beginning to end. Not to mention the specialized laboratories which were born, died, or moved elsewhere as needs changed.

The entire organism was dedicated to investigating and ascertaining the necessary facilities, equipment, and other needs of theatre and its support systems; our operation became a research prototype for the construction of workshops in future theatres. The visitors who came to our workshops and ateliers in the Flora section of Prague from all corners of the earth in those days testified to the success and relevance of this endeavor. Even a few patents emerged here. For example, the so-called contralight, which I've already touched on, is today used in practically all theatres.

One of our chief missions was to make scenography less dependent on sheer matter and traditional stage machinery. We wanted, in short, to dematerialize scenography. We achieved it in the prototypal kinetic set for Shakespeare's *Romeo and Juliet* in 1963. But this production was itself preceded by several other, seemingly diverse attempts, which were nevertheless internally related.

54

Topol. Their Day. *National Theatre, Prague, 1959. Dir: Otomar Krejča.*

The role of scenography in a theatre production is highly variable. If a text is sufficiently strong dramatically and capable of evoking an appropriate atmosphere, then the scenography should merely support it and disappear within it. At other times, on the contrary, scenography can create the foundation for necessary dramatic relations on stage and determine the atmosphere.

My first production with Otomar Krejča at the National Theatre was František Hrubín's *A Sunday in August* in 1958. During this production we all fully experienced authentic teamwork for the first time. The text emerged by degrees, systematically worked on by the entire creative collective with the author. In fact we went away together for a time to Bechyn, the locale of the action, in order to avoid distraction and to become intimately familiar with the theme and atmosphere of the play.

The hero of Hrubín's play—as we all agreed—was the atmosphere of an August day, during which all the characters become poignantly aware of what they actually want out of life, as well as what they really know about life and themselves. The scenography depicting this atmosphere was a critical factor which, while liberating the action, in some ways actually limited the director, forcing him to play almost entirely on the forestage. We consciously employed staging based on lighting. In this and other ways, *A Sunday in August* became a starting

point for further productions. It was the first time we treated projection surfaces as spatial elements.

The basis of the scenography was a raked platform covered by a neutral carpet. The rear of the raked platform was carved in such a way as to create the illusion of the shore of a pond. I experimented with concentrated lighting on two large, wedge-shaped, transparent surfaces that leaned toward each other at a forty-five degree angle and were covered by two projections. The diffused light, its oscillation, literally erased the horizontal juncture of the two surfaces. The result was an illusion of the peaceful countryside around a southern Bohemian pond, a hazy stillness, the calm of a flat terrain, and the nostalgia of late summer. The reflection of the actors and the environment on the surface of the water was achieved with a mirror. The entire performance seemed to be bathed in a silvery haze.

The director and the actors, with the help of our stage machinery specialist, Josef Kostal, knew how to work along with the scenography: they exploited our collaboration to the full, which naturally gave me great pleasure. Immediately afterward, in Tyl's *The Bagpiper from Strakonice*, we used lighting which inclined at a sharp angle *toward* the audience and transformed the actors—by their interplay with the shadows—into, among other things, rocks and trees.

In *Their Day*, by Josef Topol, in 1959, Krejča and I put

55

to use in the theatre—for the first time—the audiovisuals tested at the Brussels Expo 58. With this new production we also succeeded in taking the first step toward what had been regarded as unrealizable: we learned how to use shadow zones (i.e., zones on stage where light is consciously minimized by various technical means), and thereby raised the quality of projected images.

The play was written in the form of a film scenario with cinematic cutting and multiple, often kinetic projection screens in relation to both the actors' actions and the performance space. One of the dramatic peaks was a scene in which an auto struck down a pedestrian. His last steps on stage ending in pantomime were accompanied by two simultaneously running filmed shots. The first used a slowly tracking camera to follow the side of the road; the second followed the speeding automobile in the opposite direction. Then the penetrating sound effect of squealing brakes and tires. The pedestrian fell, the stage went to a blackout, the projected images froze, and the sound of the engine receded in the distance. Then the image of a peaceful road bordered by grassy trenches appeared on all the screens. The pedestrian, of course, lay on the forestage.

We attempted to compose multiple and differentiated visual perceptions into a new coherent picture. For example, a smaller screen moved synchronously with the actor and picked out what was needed from a projection which filled the black space of the stage. We wanted to create our effect by a composition of images and their interrelationship, and to combine this composition with the three-dimensional picture of the stage with the help of *theatrical* cuts and montages, which are similar to film cuts and montages in name only. Whatever shortcomings this scenography may have had, it served the director as a sensitive instrument and expressed what had been previously inexpressible—even though it worked only with images whose essence was movement and significant change. We were simply at the beginning, with the concomitant problems that all beginnings have.

The much discussed *Hamlet* of Jaromír Pleskot (1959) has a special position among my works. After all, it's a play that has traditionally been a touchstone for each generation. My scene was created by movable black reflective panels in five lateral rows, with light, and only the most necessary furniture. With concentration on every step, Hamlet ascended the stairs toward the nocturnal panels that bore a projected image of the royal colors. He stopped, because it was here, at this spot, that the Ghost was to speak to him.

But how to present the apparition of a ghost on the modern stage? It had to accord with an unromantic or even anti-romantic interpretation of Hamlet as presented by Radovan Lukavský. Hamlet became a sober, reflective person, a noter of facts and curber of fantasies. Hamlet stood before the dark mirror, in which were reflected two spotlights, like eyes, and at that moment we heard the Ghost speaking in Hamlet's own voice.

Originally we counted on a "natural" ghost, the old, familiar theatrical ghost. The only reason he didn't appear was simply that it was done exactly that way thirty years before! Our First Player remembered it; Eduard Kohout had played Hamlet in Hilar's and Hofman's production in 1926. Hofman was also a creator of trick effects and described

Shakespeare. Hamlet. *National Theatre, Prague, 1959. Dir: Jaromír Pleskot.*

Shakespeare. Hamlet. *National Theatre, Prague, 1959. Dir: Jaromir Pleskot.*

them in detail: "The actors wore slippers with sound absorbing felt soles; everything took place in silence, like a dream. The ghost of Hamlet's father had his naked right arm phosphorescently painted, so that it glowed under ultraviolet light even when the figure itself was invisible."

With the chief electrician at the National Theatre, we speculated and tested ad infinitum. Suddenly a chance movement of lighting instruments on the bridge, the reflection of lights from the semigloss surface of the panels—and the problem of the ghost's apparition was solved. Chance, or sudden impulse? Sometimes I ask myself, couldn't I have perceived the essence of the matter on the very first day? Once we know something, we wonder why we were blind to so many previous hints. Yet we wonder only after we know.

The scene for *Hamlet* was based on the interplay of three types of light, the prototype of which is light and shadow on a stone in nature: an intensely illuminated surface exposed to the sun, under it a deep black shadow, and at one side a half-shadow and softened light reflected from an adjacent stone. It's the prototype of any plastic form created by sharp and diffused light and reflection. Our spotlights were aimed from the front lighting bridge at twelve panels covered by a special black plastic material which had nearly fifty percent of the reflectability of a black mirror. The actors and scenic details, immersed in a uniform level of light, were simultaneously illuminated by direct and reflected light. As a result, the range of shadow values was essentially extended, hard contrasts disappeared, and forms were fuller—in the optical sense, more real. Moreover, light penetrated even to those places otherwise impossible to light.

Without going to blackouts or lowering the curtain, the scene and its lighting pattern changed twenty-four times merely by shifting the reflecting panels. Of course, for more nearly perfect work with light we would have needed more backstage space so that the sources of light could be farther removed from stage objects. Indeed, that's the only way that the geometry of the lighting could have been improved.

The twelve black reflective panels that created the scene for *Hamlet* transformed the actor into a shadowy silhouette. But how did it all relate to the Elizabethan stage? Shakespeare's theatre is a theatre of thought and dynamic acting, a theatre of precise space and time. It requires a fluidity of action. Therein lies the persistent problem of staging Shakespeare's dramas, a problem not solved by attempts at reconstructing the Elizabethan stage or the installation of stage machinery. What has always remained a problem is the flow of actions, their continuity, which only the film shot and cutting can practically achieve. But when the era of slide projections and film came to the stage in the '20s, it was clear that not even this was the answer.

We wanted to measure up to Shakespeare's direct, open playmaking—especially with regard to the conventions that Shakespeare establishes with his viewers at the beginning of each of his plays. In his opening monologue, Richard reveals all his intentions; the prologue to *Romeo and Juliet* sums up the chief problems of the play and their solution; Hamlet neatly lays out his insoluble questions before us. The play contains no hidden levels that the spectator is only supposed to uncover gradually; there is no mystery of subtexts. Active participation is expected of the viewer, who may be deliberately led astray in order to be confronted by himself a split second later. But the play must remain an open play, the stage a stage, and its space entirely determined by the dynamic relations of its characters.

The expressive principle of our scene was based on stairs that functioned as a gradually ascending surface interrupted by parallel black strips of shadow, and on mobile panels

Shakespeare. Hamlet. *National Theatre, Prague. 1959. Dir: Jaromir Pleskot.*

Chekhov. The Sea Gull. *National Theatre, Prague, 1960. Dir: Otomar Krejča.*

Photo: Jaromír Svoboda

that could change the place of action in a moment. But did the movement of the panels accomplish realistic changes of locale? Of course not. The set fulfilled a different function than the one we usually ascribe to it. It did not conventionally describe the place of action or even create it. It placed the action in absolute space, which can represent any place and any time. That is, the scene did not picture a concrete place. The movement of the abstract panels not only indicated spatial changes but was also a materialization of rhythm, by means of which the action progressed. Similar to the function of a film cut, it evoked the psychic state of the characters.

Of course, conventions of the day affect our perception. The movement of the panels could have been interpreted by some as merely abstract play and an imperfect change of the place of action. But since Shakespeare always counted on the spectator's power of fantasy, why not give it adequate opportunity? If I set out in the opposite direction, I'd end up with a mere illustration of the text. For all the pros and cons, this production of *Hamlet* was an important milestone for me. In addition to everything else, in preparing for it I came up with my principle of contralighting. And so my first encounter with Shakespeare was as it ought to be: full

of joy at the discoveries, impatience with my own limitations, and a longing to make further discoveries.

Then in 1960 came the truly risky experiment with contralights from specially designed low voltage instruments in the staging of Chekhov's and Krejča's *The Sea Gull*. If it hadn't worked, there would have been no performance; but there was no way of telling our fate until technical rehearsal.

What is a scenographer to do with Chekhov? If he steps aside and lets only the text speak, something's missing. If he starts to illustrate the plays, there's something in excess. How to capture the atmosphere in which words mean something different from what they signify anywhere else? How to create a claustrophobic space in which people are far apart? Or the sense of distance in which characters nonetheless feel close to each other?

The Sea Gull, my first Chekhov, was not born without pain. I reduced all scenographic devices to a space covered in black, with one fundamental curtain of light in the proscenium opening (tilted toward the audience and taking the place of a scrim curtain), and ten other, smaller curtains of light distributed in the depth of the stage with specially constructed low-voltage lamps with parabolic reflectors.

They were masked by twigs, through which streams of "sun" light penetrated. The resulting impression of an orchard with its sultry heat and total atmosphere, affected the spectator in a palpably physiological way.

The particular lighting hardware, the ceiling of branches with leaves of nylon netting (which did a good job of both catching the light and letting it through)—all this we conceived and worked out for the first time. Now everything depended on whether our gamble would pay off. We scoured the city for necessary parts and assembled them. Our all-night experiments were confined to the workshops; we had to wait for two days of scheduled lighting rehearsals on stage. We had no other solutions in reserve. I was in agony at the endless waiting. Indeed, from that time on I've always kept some sort of backstop solution in my pocket as an "anxiety-easer." The ultimate success of our work was a result of our team's faith in the project; they delivered professional work and, insofar as possible, left nothing to chance. The desire to get to the very essence of Chekhov's text was clearly evident in the actors' work as well. They demonstrated what it means to take off creatively from a thought-out conception of a performance into the realm of a fully realized production.

Seven years later (1967) I used a similar principle of contralighting for a production of Wagner's *Tristan and Isolde* in Wiesbaden, this time confidently, because I had already tested it. But six days before the opening it became clear to me that the principle simply wasn't working. How was it possible? Everything was the same as in Prague, except perhaps that the Germans used latex instead of glue and there was less dust on the stage. Should I have blown dust onto the stage? Nonsense. What would the singers say, and what of the authorities overseeing work safety? I tried to thicken the air with normal aerosol sprays. Their effect was temporary at best, while also generating an undesirable smoky fog that drifted about in the upper reaches of the stage. Of course, it also quickly dried out from the heat of the lighting instruments. We tried an apparatus used in factories to reduce dust by forcing water vapor into the work areas. The air did thicken a bit, but again only in the upper reaches of the stage, intermittently and unevenly; I was really desperate. It was a very costly and keenly anticipated production, and my prestige was very much at stake.

Finally, an enterprising German engineer understood what I was concerned about. He experimentally loaded the tiny fog droplets with a uniform electrostatic charge so that they were uniformly spread throughout the space. And this water vapor became the equivalent of the dustiness

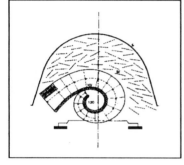

Wagner. Tristan and Isolde. *Hesse State Theatre, Wiesbaden, 1967. Dir: C.H. Drese. The groundplan shows the disposition of the lighting units. Backing the spiral ramp were sections of vertically stretched cords.*

Wagner. Tristan and Isolde. *Hesse State Theatre, Wiesbaden, 1967. Dir: C.H. Drese.*

of a Prague stage. When we no longer wanted the fog, we introduced droplets with the opposite electrostatic potential and the droplets would begin to cluster together, fall to the floor, and clear out the space. And so another production was saved by a method intended for another operation entirely.

Theatre, of course, is not always the most ideal place for experiment. It's confined by the straitjacket of the repertoire and fixed limits of time. On paper or in a model, fantastic dreams may be expressed. But only when all the personnel of a theatre want to make this dream their own, can one truly begin. And so in every theatre two groups of people are absolutely essential: those who conceive, and those who actualize. The great challenge is to bring together fellow workers from entirely different professions who speak the same language.

We had progressed somewhat farther down this road later in 1960, once more with Otomar Krejča, in Tyl's *Drahomíra*. In this instance I was concerned with a contrary phenomenon: the *absorption* of light. Its reflection from the floor of the stage had a negative effect since it heightened the level of parasitic light. (Without this unexpected consequence, on the other hand, I wouldn't have been prepared later to solve the scenic challenge of Lorca's *The House of Bernarda Alba*.) In *Drahomíra* I simply hadn't counted on the reflected light changing the floor of the stage for me. The effect was so distracting that it threatened the quality of the whole work. The great intensity of the light streaming from the low voltage sources resulted in excessive illumination of the floor, which, though covered by a black carpet, was not capable of absorbing the light. The surface of the carpet became gray, allowing the spectator to detect every stitch and nail in it. We experimented with a variety of materials but without any positive result. Not until two years later did we succeed in finding a material with low, in fact, directional reflectibility.

The scenography for *Drahomíra* did benefit from one defect: dust. The carpet accumulated so much dust, which was drawn away by the flow of air heated by the lighting instruments, that it proceeded to saturate the atmosphere. This gave the curtains of light a splendid silvery sheen that we never could have planned in advance.

Director Krejča and I agreed that Tyl's drama of pagan times could be presented with an historical atmosphere but have its primary impact as a great contemporary drama of human passions and the never resolved clash between tradition and new ways of relating to the world. The stage was enclosed by distinctively aged wooden boards. It also had a curtain, not of draperies but of three wooden rectangles; the curtain had a dramatic function, which was heightened by lighting shaped by masks. The mobile construction rose at the beginning of each act to reveal a view of empty space and a monumental raked platform also in the form of a rectangle with access stairs cut into its sides. Smaller triangular platforms could tilt up from its surface to provide special acting areas.

In the final scene, in which Prince Václav breaks away from the interests of the people, the largest of the rectangles tilted forward ninety degrees and formed a ceiling over the front part of the stage. Sharp, intense light struck its upper surface and created darkness beneath it, swallowing up the figure of Václav. But as soon as it was lit from the front it began to glow, becoming almost phosphorescent. After his dialogue with Václav, as old Popel was departing, the wooden rectangle of the roof slowly returned to its original position. Václav found himself facing a high wall, which separated him from Popel. Then two more rectangles were lowered behind him and cut him off from the audience. That was the last of Václav. The director made use of the space offered to him to its fullest potential, and the production revealed Josef Kajetan Tyl as a great Czech dramatist.

The scenography for Sophocles' *Oedipus*, directed by Miroslav Macháček in 1963, led to an unexpected risk. It involved nothing but a staircase, which filled the entire width of the stage and stretched up from the orchestra pit to a height of

Tyl. Drahomíra. *National Theatre, Prague, 1960. Dir: Otomar Krejča.*

Sophocles. Oedipus. National Theatre, Prague, 1963. Dir: Miroslav Macháček. The final scene of the play. An orchestra accompanied the action from under the stairs; in order for it to be heard properly, the risers of the stairs were made of acoustically "transparent" material.

15 meters. All the reproaches I've had from critics about my staircases! The attacks on me for repeating myself! But after all, a person can't abandon a road until he feels that he's come to the end of it and discovered its last secret. That secrets still remain for me in lighting is tolerated by the critics. But in stairs? They'll never stop exciting me, any more than I'll one day become bored with Jacob's ladder or Icarus's wings.

The end of *Oedipus* always frightened me. Where does Oedipus go? Abandoned by everyone, he goes in search of truth, even though he knows it will destroy him. He wants to do good, though he now realizes the futility of battling fate. In spite of everything, he goes, bent over, dragging himself up the stairs. The audience can read his back and sense his misery. Only stairs could express all this to me.

A few platforms on the giant staircase occasionally changed their positions. An eighty-five member orchestra was positioned under the stairs. In order to assure clear audibility of the sound, each riser of the stairs was perforated. But when all of these provisions had been beautifully calculated, we were still confronted with the problem of how to construct the stairs so that they could be set up and then struck after each performance within standard time limits. There were many who anticipated that this time I'd certainly fail. But the Hořejš-Frey duo wouldn't quit until they put together a construction out of small modules that could be assembled and disassembled

like an erector set. And they demonstrated that it could be done within the allotted time. The critics' reproach was that in this instance the actors were serving the scenography. But I'm convinced that given the director's concept, the opposite was in fact true.

Like staircases, cycloramas have also continued to tantalize me over the years. At the same time, especially in our country, it has often been thrown up to me that I've come up with nothing new at all. I simply continue to play with cycloramas! I suspended the cyclorama above the floor for the first time in *Dalibor* and then in Shakespeare's *Henry V* (1971)—and let the actors walk beneath it. All the furniture and props could be seen; the business with them was part of the blocking. In Sheridan's *The School for Scandal* (1972) director Macháček wanted no scene changes. I made an interior, three walls, doors left and right. Each wall, stretched over a 20 centimeter thick frame, was also a projection screen for rear projections. For acoustical reasons, the same arrangement applied to the ceiling.

The room was suspended a little above the turntable in the stage floor. Right away we were faced with an embarrassing problem. The doors weren't large enough to get the furniture inside. Very unhappy, I sat long into the night at Flora, staring at the model. Suddenly I realized that the tallest piece of furniture was 120 centimeters. I picked up a pair of scissors and cut 120 centimeters from the bottom of the room. Now the turntable could turn and the needed furniture would ride merrily along on it. It's simply necessary to follow each problem through to its logical end.

In *Our Hotheads* (1979), again with director Miroslav Macháček, the cyclorama was also hung above the floor,

Shakespeare. Henry V. *National Theatre, Prague, 1971. Dir: Miroslav Macháček.*

creating the illusion of the sky outlining the silhouette of the village. The cyclorama sky had its lower edge cut in the form of the skyline of the village, leaving empty black space beneath to allow furniture behind the cyclorama to be brought on and off like props. During all these experiments with cycloramas I was becoming aware of their possibilities for ballet.

I took advantage of those possibilities for the first time in the scenography-in-a-suitcase for *Swan Lake* in 1982 for Milan's La Scala (which I'll touch on later). I would explore the possibilities further when I worked with Roland Petit in 1985 on the ballet *Professor Unrat* (libretto by Heinrich Mann) for the Deutsche Opera in Berlin. The cyclorama drew the silhouette of Lübeck; it is no mean feat to make a silhouette become a sign. The specific material I chose was Gerriets's blue folio[1] "Bluesky." Unfortunately, this folio was not available, and

a substitute was sent instead. We were using frontal projection, and also using contralights; the folio was to be translucent and give off a dark blue glow. As soon as I saw the substitute material, I knew it wouldn't hang right; folds would be inevitable. It looked awful, like a puttee rag. It was risk time yet again. My friend Walter Gerriets agreed to produce the desired folio within a week. I designed its form and cut it. The gamble paid off. The folio hung like a charm. So, whatever anyone may think, as long as adventures keep presenting themselves up stairs or along cycloramas, I intend to pursue them.

When Otomar Krejča picked *Romeo and Juliet* for the 1963 season, our experience with Pleskot's *Hamlet* taught us what questions to ask. Why perform this particular work at this particular time? And given appropriate answers, how to justify them on stage? In response to the director's concept, I elected architecture as the basis for the scenography. The architecture was to be dynamic and move in space. I wanted to employ the modulating distances between actors and setting as dramatic elements to create new relations within the play. I would handle the space with consistent cleanness and precision. No aesthetic tricks allowed.

It was architecture that hid within it a model of the human world. It didn't seek to amaze one with its beauty, but rather with its calm and simplicity, its precise proportions and style. The degree of precision was evident in the loggia, which was to appear to float in the air. At the same time, of course, its specifications had to guarantee absolute safety in terms of materials and construction, and its internal structural tensions couldn't prompt any unforeseen movement, oscillation from the axis, or fracturing where its sole support touched the floor.

But is wasn't only a matter of kinetic architecture; its individual elements also had to be transformable. For example, the fountain wasn't merely a meeting place for the youth of Verona; it was also transformed into the lovers' wedding-night bed as well as their tomb. The contralight invested Juliet's loggia, that gliding love craft, with a special, near spiritual purity and light of Renaissance paintings. For basic materials we used burlap and wood, but the lighting changed them into sandstone. With this production the collective at Flora proved itself extraordinarily capable. *Romeo and Juliet* would be my most precise scenic and technical work up to that time. A short instructional film was made of the preparations, so that all personnel involved would know what was waiting for them. Even with the benefit of hindsight I wouldn't change a single detail.

Brecht's *Mother Courage* (1970), which I prepared with director Jan Kačer for the National Theatre, was another of our high-risk gambles. The scene was created by an irregularly shaped, crumpled piece of rusted, gouged metal some 14 meters across and as thick as a half meter at some points. This strange flying saucer weighed three tons and was suspended above the stage from three ten-millimeter cables. Each cable had its own fly-line hoist so the pan could freely move into a variety of positions. Its undersurface of brilliantly shining metal was a symbol of the enticements of war, recruiting, the promise of victory and jolly parades. Its rusty and blood soaked upper surface

Brecht. Mother Courage. *National Theatre, Prague, 1970. Dir: J. Kacer. The top surface of the sheetmetal mass tilted toward the audience. The crumpled, torn, corroded surface represented the battlescarred earth.*

was a grim reminder of war's reality. For Katrin the metal became a drum, on which she sounded her alarm. Finally, an exhausted Mother Courage herself—the excellent Dana Medřická—re-attached a wheel that had come off and dragged the wagon over the uneven surface of the pan. The battered metal rattled and resounded. Imagine the extreme security measures we had to take with three tons constantly hanging over the actors' heads! But we accomplished it.

I admit I had subconsciously avoided Brecht all my life. Then one day in 1972 the intendant of the Zurich theatre offered me *The Threepenny Opera.* I was truly at a loss. The usual approach to doing Brecht all over the world didn't appeal to me. But because of Brecht's very potent author-centered tradition, I feared that any diversion from it would be condemned. Moreover, Karl von Appen had honorably sustained that tradition. For *The Threepenny Opera,* he hung an orchestra above the rear of the stage, where it would be visible throughout the performance. His forestage with a low curtain was perfect. The curtain was, in fact, the crucial element. How was I to get the songs in front of the curtain and yet not copy Appen? The only flaw in his solution was that the conductor was placed behind the actors, with his back to the audience. But I had done that, too, in Prokofiev's *The Love for Three Oranges* (1963).

I had that unhappy curtain constantly before my eyes. Of course, what everybody expected from me were projections. But if I wanted the songs in front of the curtain, I had to have a curtain! But how would the actors get through this curtain? Then one day while waiting at the Frankfurt airport for my luggage I happened to notice how the suitcases rode into the waiting room on a moving belt through a vertically sliced curtain. Before my valise arrived, I knew I had my answer. I hung a curtain of folio material for frontal and rear projection from a midway position, like a pendulum. As the curtain swung back from the extreme downstage position, it carried a frontally projected image until the central cross-fading point, at which moment a second, rear projected image faded up to form the background of the scenography while the actors walked through the sliced-up folio. The cross-fade was so subtle that no one was capable of realizing how it came about. Actually, the panel strips of the curtain had a good "memory" and instantly returned to their original positions.

The greatest collective is still made up of individuals. We had no shortage of individuals, including engineers Schwarz and Hamouž, Miroslav Pflug, and Zdeněk Minář.

Wherever individual personalities converge and discussions begin, tranquil harmony is not likely to ensue. We lived through hundreds of these confrontations of opinion and plain squabbles. How often we swore never to work with each other again! But the collective also confirmed its identity with these explosions. They revealed actual, substantive problems; and the conflicts led to solutions. In such a collective, it was impossible to twist substantive disputes into personal ones. Workers often came to us from one workshop or another earnestly declaring that a certain job could not be done as quickly as we had expected. But we knew precisely the extent of our demands; if they hadn't been realistic we wouldn't have made them. After explaining our reasoning, we usually saw our original wishes and schedule prevail. But there were some hot encounters!

Our collective at Flora was the natural group to prepare the Czechoslovak pavillion in Brussels and Montreal in 1958 and 1967. There was simply no other workplace with as high a standard. Our sustained, purposeful, and socially useful work further fortified the sense of responsibility of the collective and its individuals. It did, however, take twenty years for us to perfect an insider's shorthand. By that time we were so familiar with our respective points of view that we could transact an entire conversation with a glance or a few words.

Running the Flora operations consumed roughly forty percent of my total time those days. Many people say it was time that might have been better spent on my own work. They're not right. Regardless of the events that led to my leaving Flora, I'll never regret those years of commitment. In fact, there's nothing else I could have done

Shakespeare. Romeo and Juliet. *National Theatre, Prague, 1963. Dir: Otomar Krejča.*

and still be what I am. Moreover, those very years made possible the broad spectrum of my work. My progress as an artist and technician was shaped by the relentless course of creative challenges posed for me at Flora. And I am grateful for each and every one of those challenges, as I am grateful to all my fellow workers of those days in the workshops of the National Theatre—the living and the dead, wherever they are.[2]

When I look back on my meeting with Alfred Radok during the war, I realize that no other meeting in my life resembled it. We did things together that would have been utterly impossible without the absolute accord of perception and vision that we enjoyed. Our occasional long separations never interrupted the collegial and spiritual understanding we shared. In each instance, we were able to pick up our work together as if we had never parted. Regrettably, these gaps meant that we did much less together than we might have done.

In 1948, when we had already done Maeterlinck's *The Mayor of Stilmond* in the drama wing of Theatre of the Fifth of May and several productions in the Satire Theatre, the National Theatre entrusted us with Lillian Hellman's *The Little Foxes*. We tried to place this excellent text into the most appropriate and least distracting setting. The set consisted of a room with a ceiling, a floor, and two walls; since one was missing, the carpet ran on to where it was no longer visible. Similarly, a staircase with a landing actually didn't end. Nothing here had an end, yet the end of everything was here.

We didn't work together again until 1955, in the National Theatre production of *The Devil's Circle* by Hedy Zinner. It was more nearly a radio play, but its real-life source—Giorgi Dmitrov's Leipzig trial stemming from the 1933 Reichstag fire—provoked us to point out, ten years after the war, those signs of fascism that were being forgotten despite random and simplified official reminders.

We had nothing on stage except what was strictly demanded by the dramatic action, its atmosphere and expressiveness. We loosely assembled the individual scenes and their scenic elements, carefully relating elements of bare reality with stylized expressiveness. Radok proved beyond any doubt his ability to transform a topical piece into a devastating, very human message.

Two years later we tackled *The Golden Carriage* by Leonid Leonov. The fate of people in a small Russian town right after the war—including the chairwoman of the town soviet, a demobilized colonel, a boy who lost his sight at the front, an old Muslim whose family was murdered by the Nazis, and others—grew by means of Radok's concept and the actors' interpretations into a passionate indictment of war and a celebration of people who never forget their responsibility, whatever the circumstances.

I tried to bring onto the stage a feeling of interminable distances and endless suffering. I used pure space without masking, with no theatrical clichés, bordered only by fog. Furniture tightly squeezed in small islands either in the proscenium opening or in the middle of the stage called up the impression of ruins; a wash basin into which water dripped, a feeling of misery. Other than the furniture and stoves, I used only doors, through which the actors entered. They were brought behind the doors by an elevator, for we wanted sight of no other entry. Everything on stage served to evoke the unrelenting atmosphere from which the production then developed a ballad of those who survived the war.

In 1957 Radok and I returned once again to Lillian Hellman, in her *Autumn Garden*. I built a commonplace room of an American house with a terrace, naturalistic down to the very last prop. But then I painted everything on the stage mouse gray. With one stroke I had an abstract space, which in fact functioned like a cyclorama. The colorful costumes of the actors and a bouquet that was brought on stage were utterly unable to overcome this pervasive grayness. Of course the grayness of life inexorably won out.

Our third work together that same year was Osborne's *The Entertainer*. It was as if we had returned to our earliest days together with this production. We had a story that allowed us to evoke universally familiar, emotionally experienced life situations and treat them in a poetic, non-illustrational manner. The production was an extraordinary success thanks both to Ladislav Pešek's performance as the main character, Archie Rice, and to our consistent use of readily understandable signs in conveying the story on stage.

One example was the method we used to present the funeral of Archie's father, Billy Rice. Billy customarily stopped at the old upright player piano, which he cheated by attaching a string to the coin he deposited. As ever, Billy tosses in the coin, and the piano starts the old favorite, "Good Night, Ladies..." Billy bows and goes to lie down. One of several little sequinned curtains closes behind him. The piano tune is taken over by a live orchestra, and Archie Rice steps in front of the curtain, gesturing and smiling as if he wants to start his number. Instead, he stops the music and announces that Billy Rice will not perform today. The sequinned curtain opens again, slowly, as if in a crematorium, then another behind it, and another. Archie doffs his top hat; behind him stands his assembled family, as if waiting for something. The silence is interrupted only by the sound of someone hammering a nail. Two men with straps on their shoulders step out from behind the proscenium arch, go to the piano, and expertly carry it to the edge of the stage, like professional movers. A clock strikes. Archie stands motionless, with his hat off. And then the men start to lower the piano into the orchestra pit, as if lowering a coffin into a grave. The members of the orchestra stand. The silence persists; the only sound comes

Osborne. The Entertainer. *National Theatre, Prague, 1957. Dir: Alfred Radok. Svoboda's drawing reveals the main components of the setting.*

from the piano as it grazes the walls of the orchestra pit before settling on the floor. Then a murmur from the orchestra pit as the musicians sit down and start to get ready for the next number.

At the end of the play, ten revue curtains ran on trolley wires. As Archie, a totally washed up comedian, made his final, broken exit, blue, red, yellow, and purple little curtains opened successively before him, their colors and movement in striking contrast to Archie's movement and manner, creating the feeling of a wordless and yet entirely convincing tragic end.

I made many sketches for the scenography. Finally, we reduced the setting to a nocturnal, foggy street with streetlamps, a clock with three faces, and trolley wires. The interior was represented by three walls and furniture. The third wall receded upstage, as needed, and the other two to the sides; each had lace wallpaper with trophies attached. A stylized bistro could be brought on to the street as well as into the interior. The bistro's curtains rode in along the trolley wires, the movement of the curtains requiring split-second precision from the stage technicians. Everything on the stage, like the piano, had its own dramatic role and worked together in concert.

After the Brussels Expo of 1958, where we developed the Laterna Magika system, Radok and I would work together only once more (other than on Lorca's *House of Bernarda Alba*). In 1966 at the National Theatre our collaboration on *The Last Ones* by Maxim Gorky drew on Laterna Magika techniques and produced our most important work in discovering further expressive possibilities for theatre—possibilities not used to this day. We knew that if we wanted to reveal what we found in Gorky's play we had to proceed as we did in the Laterna: we had to write a scenario.

At the time, in his foreword to his adaptation of the play, Radok noted, "Some of the means used by the production are illogical in terms of life probability. But it's possible to accept them on an emotional level. A dual, contradictory action will often be occurring on several levels. For instance, on the stage and in the film, in the text and in the music that accompanies the text. This multiplicity of relationships presupposes work from the actors that has several levels of meaning. By means of this emphasis on the complex and truthful work of the actors, this production is able to resonate with the audience of 1966."

The entire production was systematically built on harsh antitheses: the thoroughly disagreeable incidents occurring in the family of the police official Ivan Kolomijcev took place in the constant presence of a festive little band which played familiar pieces from promenade concerts. All the scenographic

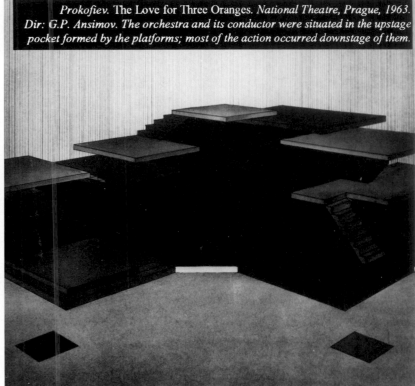

elements on stage were subordinated to the relationship between stage and film. Because music was an independent dramatic element, a substantial loge for the band was built into the large projection screen that formed most of the rear wall. The loge was situated directly behind the upper part of the screen and was alternately closed off or revealed. The result was a collage of several realities: the gray walls of the loge with chandeliers and a small theatrical curtain; several doors, a cracked upright piano, a torn folding screen behind which was hidden a bed, a table, and a wheelchair. And finally a door appeared and disappeared from behind the proscenium arch at one side of the raked stage.

All this was concentrated toward one goal: to expose the emptiness and falsity of the grandiloquent words—love, family, country, "all that is holy to us"—so lavishly used by Ivan Kolomijcev. After the opening night, critics spoke of our providing the audience with excessive "technocratic abundance," and of the director's use of methods already quite familiar, altered or in fact simply copied from his previous work in theatre, film, and Laterna Magika. Quite simply, he was branded a plagiarist of his own work. At the time I recalled a sentence from a film about Hemingway: "If all you know is addition, don't suspect the results of a person who multiplies just because he gets different results with the same numbers."

And that was precisely the relationship between Laterna Magika and Radok's production of *The Play of Love and Death* in the Komorní Theatre and *The Last Ones*. In *The Play of Love and Death* (1964) Radok used Rolland's non-dramatic text as the source for a dramatic composition which in performance thoroughly harmonized with the source. With Gorky's *The Last Ones* he demonstrated that one could consider similar source material from a different, in fact, opposite, angle, to achieve the same result. The perspective of *The Play of Love and Death* developed from

a multitude of characters distributed among actors, singers, and dancers, who were brought together and into focus in Ladislav Vychodil's unambiguous and stable set.[3] In *The Last Ones*, on the contrary, the focal point became the dramatic figures, each of whom was narrowed to one single psychological sign or abstract trait, in which the multiple aspects of the scenography could converge. Here, the chief roles were played by Pretense, Suffering Womankind, Naiveté, Calculation, Self-Love, Debauchery, and Appetite.

The critics also complained of forced expressive compression. "Forced compression" and "technocratic abundance." It's an obvious contradiction, and I mention it now, after many years, only because it involved more than mere misunderstanding or incomprehension. We were concerned with developing a method for our work in the future.

The production had a scene in which Vera, the youngest daughter of police official Kolomijcev, yields to Jakorevov. It's not in the original text of the play; it was added to enable the audience to appreciate their intimate relationship. The audience also became aware of the polonaise that is part of Vera's dream of love. We then hit the audience with a sharp cut to the repeated screen image of a street skirmish and the volley shot at Sokolov, a fleeing student. When this screen image changed into a suggestion of an execution scene, the stage action beneath the screen showed the maids (an ever present chorus) surrounding the lovers. At the end of the scene, other servants lifted the bed as if it were a coffin and bore it away. Although *The Last Ones* prompted allusions to technocratic abundance and expressionistic compression, reference could as easily have been made to symbolism. Certain moments created a symbolic parallel so graphic that no further speculation was required. At the same time that Nadezdina's bare back was gently stroked by maids with birch twigs during a live scene, we projected a larger than life screen image of a prisoner's bare back being

individual elements of this production, then indeed there could have been a feeling of surfeit and superfluity. The director had laid a series of charges under the text of Gorky's play, charges composed of contrapuntal elements that detonated at precisely timed intervals. These intervals shaped the underlying structural pattern of the production, contracting or expanding its zone of action. We were setting up a confrontation of memory with the present, a confrontation between the spectator's experience at the moment of performance with his experiences in the past, now awakened by the performance.

Just one or two more examples. In the second act, Vera and Jakorevov dance onto the stage— we're at a ball. A chandelier is lowered, the loge is revealed, and the band plays. The ballroom space is outlined by black-garbed men with white gloves. Between dances, Jakorevov strolls with Vera, describing his heroic shooting

whipped while he was pinioned to a stone wall. Or another symbol: while the maids giggled, the nurse laid a bare sword on Vera's wedding bed and Vera knocked down a tailor's mannequin dressed in her wedding gown.

If one failed to sense the resonating significance of the

Strindberg. The Dream Play.
*State University of New York
at Albany, 1980.
Dir: Jarka Burian.*

Strauss. Ariadne auf Naxos.
National Arts Center, Ottawa, 1977.
Dir: Václav Kašlik.

Gorky. The Last Ones. *National Theatre, Prague, 1966. Dir: Alfred Radok*

Photo: Jaromír Svoboda

of Sokolov. His words are accompanied by a documentary-type film sequence of Jakorevov shooting Sokolov that absolutely contradicts his narrative.

The performance ends with Vera's return from Jakorevov. She has now been robbed of all illusions. She tears off her clothes and throws them away as if they were soiled. Once again we hear the music of the ball; the chandelier descends, and on the screen we review the reality of Jakorevov's "heroism." The music dies down, the curtain of the loge starts to close, and the chandelier dims down and ascends. Vera wraps herself in the blanket and seeks refuge in her mother's arms.

The filmed images reprised throughout the production became signals that gave the stage incidents a new, dialectic significance; in turn, the images acquired a renewed significance by contrast with the stage action. The setting in and of itself was an indeterminate collage, the function of which was clarified as the action progressed, establishing the point of view of time, on whose dramatic armature the entire production of *The Last Ones* was composed.

More than twenty years have flowed by since the premiere of *The Last Ones*; and it's now been several years since Radok's death. Have we progressed since that time? I see no positive answer. And so nothing remains but for me to say to Radok—thanks, and may the earth rest lightly on you.

Opposite: Mozart. The Marriage of Figaro. *National Theatre, Prague, 1961. Dir: Karel Jernek. Photo: Jaromír Svoboda*

OPERA

As a young man I thought of opera as theatre of the past—certainly beautiful if sung beautifully, but nonetheless irretrievably gone. I wanted to do theatre that addressed people the very day they witnessed it—a contemporary theatre, and of course, a theatre of the future. Opera had no role in my life.

Needless to say, my first productions at the Theatre of the Fifth of May were naturally—what else—operas! But in those days, which were personally so happy for me, everything became an adventure that made our heads spin. Even opera became exciting. We soon realized that although the musical scores to opera had already been discovered, the way of staging them had not.

My greatest discovery about opera was that one did not stage the libretto at all. One's first and enduring obligation is to stage the music. This recognition first startled, then overwhelmed me. Ultimately, it liberated me. A confusing libretto ceased to be unduly oppressive. The directorial and design activity centered on the music. And we approached the music with modesty; after all, it carried within itself a message that didn't require help in coming to life. It did mean learning to understand the music; how to read a piano score; how to grasp the principle of phrasing—as well as the potentialities and dangers of thematic repetitions.

However—although opera is primarily music, it is not *only* music. Opera is theatre, theatre of the highest possible stylization; in fact it is stylization of stylization. Its own essence makes it impossible to be any sort of direct reflection of reality. It either gravitates toward universal issues of life and death, or else it takes as its subject an anecdotal story.

It's rather difficult to sing of contemporary themes, since even contemporary opera so often reaches back to the past for its subject matter, even while viewing it through contemporary eyes. One of the welcome characteristics of opera is that it blatantly disregards the logic of time and place, allowing those who stage it the same freedom. It makes time so relative that a mere moment of thematic repetition may force us to consider the significance of that moment again and again.

Take death, for example. As we all know, death occurs very often in opera. A brief obituary makes the point: Caravadossi and Tosca, Mimi in *La Boheme*, Violetta in *Traviata*, and Lensky in *Onegin*; Carmen, Salome, Siegfried, Tannhauser, Rusalka and the Prince, and so on and so on. And through their singing—as if we were with them—we cross the threshold of the eternal unknown, that which lies beyond everything we know, the threshold of the fourth dimension. Deaths certainly occur more often in operas than in plays, with the possible exception of Shakespeare and some of his contemporaries. We become aware, each time, how death clings inseparably to our lives.

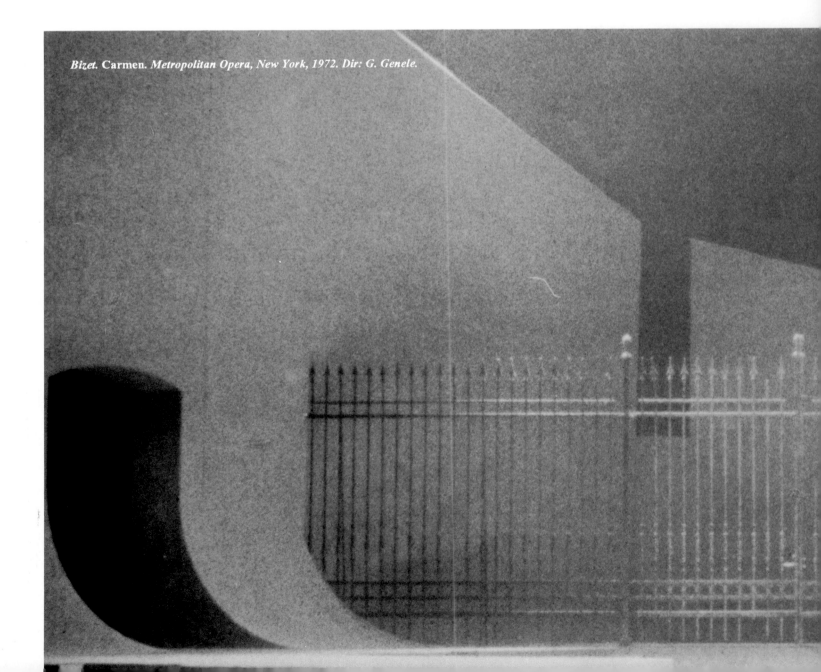

Bizet. **Carmen.** *Metropolitan Opera, New York, 1972. Dir: G. Genele.*

Puccini. Tura**n**dot. *Grand Theatre, Geneva, 1976. Dir: J. C. Riber.*

Yet it is as though singing eased this recognition for us. The obsessive exploration of this realm may be the reason why opera, so often declared dead, will never lack enthusiastic audiences nor lose its allure.

For a designer, opera provides great opportunities and severe challenges. The designer has to arouse the spectator's fantasy without ever coercing it. He mustn't compel him to a conclusion, but merely act as a catalyst to a

gradual revelation by means of precise suggestions. He provides the atmosphere for a solo or a choral passage, but must himself remain invisible. The designer must achieve an intangible effect by tangible means. And the means must be those of theatre, not reality.

In my most important opera productions abroad, I worked most often with the German director Götz Friedrich, the longtime collaborator of Walter Felsenstein. We met for the first time during Bizet's *Carmen* in Bremen in 1965. Here was another director, after Kašlík and Radok, with whom I immediately discovered a mutual alphabet, a mutual language.

The sheer variety of ways to interpret Bizet's *Carmen*! As a picture book of Spain for tourists, as a bittersweet story that merely connects perennially fresh arias... Our *Carmen* lashed together passion and an unbridled desire for liberty. Song functioned as an erotic magnet in this drama which must inexorably end in death.

In terms of design, my starting point was the smugglers' scene in the mountains. The style of this scene often seems to deviate from the style of the overall production, but from this scene I was determined to make a universal environment for everything else: the scene in front of the factory, the tavern, the arena and its spectators. I built an x-shaped construction of stairs without risers up to a height of twelve meters, consisting of an inclined section of wooden planks that intersected with an oppositely inclined section. The audience could easily see through this entire structure. In the final scene the chorus with their colorful scarves covered these stairs, sat on them with their backs to the audience, and thus created the effect of an arena that awaits the toreador's victory. Both protagonists then stood on stage confronting each other, dazed by erotic desire.

A second *Carmen*, which I did in 1972 at the Metropolitan Opera in New York with director Goran Gentele, had a still more distinctive social character. A burning sun dominated the noon break in front of the tobacco factory. The air was motionless; the exhausted, resigned women workers rested on bales of tobacco in the only shade they could find. No one was in direct light; everyone was annihilated by the heat and by dull boredom. And at this moment of a phantasmic high noon, Carmen began her dance and song, like a challenge to the limitless apathy around her, her manifestation of indomitable vitality, which finally provokes violence and crime.

I put together the scene for this *Carmen* solely with light. I used 150,000 more watts than usual for a theatre performance. It was so hot on stage that we had to install special air conditioning. The light was so intense that we painted some walls black to make them appear white and not blindingly dazzling. I composed the architecture of the space in such a way as to interrupt and break up the light in various ways. At the very end of the opera, Carmen, in white, stood by a brilliantly white wall; opposite her, in black, stood Don Jose, with a bloody stain on his costume. And in that harsh light, Carmen was simply consumed as if in a white-hot furnace.

I worked a second time with Götz Friedrich in 1966 on Verdi's *Trovatore* at the Comic Opera in East Berlin. Verdi's themes reach all the way back to Sophocles. Most

Bizet Carmen. *Theater am Goetheplatz, Bremen, 1965. Dir: Götz Friedrich.*

often they show an individual longing for his life's fulfillment in conflict with the machinery of society. He finds himself in situations that he had set up in good faith, with good intentions; but the result is the exact opposite. Verdi's themes portray the paradox of human endeavor in an inhuman world.

The fundamental thesis of *Trovatore* might be compressed into a single biblical sentence: "Cain, where is your brother, Abel?" The opera presents a medieval, harshly divided world, very evocative of the present. Ten years after the East Berlin uprising, the hero of our production was the echo of that rebellion—and its suppression.

I put two square-shaped platforms on stage, measuring 8 x 8 meters, partially lying across one another; each one had its own tower, which turned with the platform. It was a space suggesting the fateful determination of the two brothers, dual four-sided imprisonment. As supplementary architectonic material I used nothing but lights without any sort of projection. Areas of light and darkness gave the account the tone of an eternal story.

Still in that same year, 1966, Friedrich and I were confronted by a very thankless task. Because we had used up a truly large sum of money on the production of *Carmen* in Bremen, we received an amount generally regarded as laughable for the Bremen production of Mozart's *Don Giovanni*, this opera of operas!

Whenever I hear the word opera, Mozart comes to mind. He must have composed as easily as other people talk, or as Picasso painted. With that very same surge and shocking concreteness he seizes on the most ordinary concept and makes of it a unique and absolutely vital human story. A separate chapter could be devoted to the relation between the music of Mozart's operas and the text of the librettos. His librettos, although not bad as a whole, are still less important than those of other authors. Mozart's music, which speaks by itself, directly, with immediacy, makes it virtually impossible to misinterpret the stage action or character relationships.

Orff. Prometheus. *Staatsoper, Munich, 1968. Dir: August Everding.*

Wagner. The Flying Dutchman. *Smetana Theatre, Prague, 1959. Dir: Václav Kašlik.*

Mozart. Don Giovanni. *National Theatre, Prague, 1962. Dir: Václav Kašlick.*

Mozart. Don Giovanni. *Operntheater, Bremen, 1966. Dir: Götz Friedrich.*

Now we stood before a masterwork like *Don Giovanni* with the budget for a banal comedy. I needed to devise the right space for the deep stage in Bremen, a space in which we wanted to emphasize the ironic and absurd aspects of the work; to make a mysterium in revue form.

We performed without a curtain; all changes occurred on an open stage. The performance space was a huge two-part chessboard with three inner proscenium openings. At the beginning of the performance all the chess pieces were tightly clustered in the depth of the stage. The actors were on the forestage, with the spectators opposite them. Don Giovanni was a proud hero without a name. The chess action was handled by the ballet, which shifted the chess pieces and removed them as soon as they had fulfilled their function, as if the ballet were following the laws of a fateful chess match. The chess pieces themselves were designed as functional and decorative sculpted pieces (for example, a small bench, a fountain, and so on). The last piece to remain on the chessboard was the Commandant's statue.

Where I painstakingly sought a universal space for the Bremen *Don Giovanni*, I was intent on just the opposite effect in the 1969 Prague production directed by Kašlík. We had at our disposal the Tyl theatre,[1] which turned out to be a decisive factor since it had been in this very theatre that Mozart himself conducted the opera for the first time. We did everything to recreate Mozart's celebrated premiere of

Don Giovanni. We created a veritable Pragensis, or salute to Prague, chiefly by creating on stage a mirror image of the Tyl theatre's eighteenth-century auditorium loges. Precisely because the spirit of the place was firmly anchored in it, the production emphasized still other facets of the work which in their own way emerged as stylistically compact and clean as they did in the Bremen version.

Uncreative stereotypes have always irritated me; one of them is the way people usually stage Mozart's *Idomeneo*, with a painterly approach. Kašlík and I had our first experience with the work in Vienna in 1971. The scene was based on half of a baroque ceiling in the shape of a U, inclined from the floor at an angle of forty-five degrees away from the viewer. The normal sculpted decor framing the ceiling was replaced by the chorus, which moved along its edges on a staircase. A suspended mirror formed a right angle with the open end of the ceiling, thereby optically completing the ceiling and its sculpted decor as one straight plane. The area within the frame was changed by simple scenographic means and projections.

I would tackle *Idomeneo* once more, again with Kašlík, in 1981. The basis of this Canadian production was a cube 7 x 7 x 7 meters, the front surface of which I modelled into Poseidon's face. I divided the piece into five vertical sections, each 1.4 meters wide, with the nose in the middle section. When facing front, the complete face functioned

Mozart. Idomeneo. *Staatsoper, Vienna, 1971. Dir: Václav Kašlik.*

Mozart's music is like a beacon that calls on all those who are involved with the operas to realize that they have in their hands one of the supreme creations of the human spirit. I felt a similarly urgent challenge before the 1971 production of Berg's *Wozzek* in Milan. Concurrent with Berg's opera in La Scala, I was also working at the Piccola Scala on Büchner's drama of the same name; both productions were directed by Virginio Puecher. What's *Wozzek* about? The search for the meaning of human destiny. Of course, not in the direct and inexorable encounters of classical tragedy, but in the fleeting yet equally inexorable moments of everyday life.

Wozzek's own story was played as if in the real world; the scenography attempted to indicate his everyday human level. The foundation of the scene was a mirrored space with mirrored panels suggesting the skyline of a large city. Backing up the mirrors like an encompassing cyclorama were panels of special folios designed for rear projections (e.g., images of the cosmos). The individual scenes were played out on independent satellites running on tracks on the stage floor. These satellites, in the spirit of the play, either approached each other, moved apart, or met. The quite provocative result suggested the atmosphere of a tragedy of our time. I had previously tried to achieve a more concrete version of this atmosphere in substance and form in productions of the operas *Intolleranza* by Luigi Nonna and *The Soldiers* by Bernd-Alois Zimmermann.

The epic core of *Intolleranza* is the return of an emigrant to his native land and his senseless death during a flood. The most distinctive feature of its music is its attempt to capture the nervous pulse of the sounds that envelope us in today's world. The opera had its premiere in Italy in 1961, when Kašlik and I presented it in the Teatro La Fenice in Venice. Later, I was invited to collaborate on its 1965

somewhat as a proscenium curtain. Its five vertical pieces separated for the various scenes, sliding smoothly and quietly on the glossy floor. We evoked atmosphere by means of projections onto the cyclorama behind the sculpted pieces: fire, water, and so on. Even though I came quite close to what I wanted with this second *Idomeneo*, I still have the feeling that there's something more in *Idomeneo* that I have not yet discovered.

Mozart. Idomeneo. *National Arts Center, Ottawa, 1981. Dir: Václav Kašlik.*

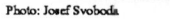

production in Boston with director Sarah Caldwell.

In the Boston theatre I was able to put my hands on equipment and facilities that I previously could only dream about. Part of the dream was industrial television with the possibility and capability of instantly reproducing whatever was being shot. In preparing the production, we had the cooperation of the Massachusetts Institute of Technology and Channel Two of Boston television. We had three projection screens on stage. The center one showed filmed sequences related to the action on stage; at each side was a 4 x 6 meter screen that could receive live video images from two Eidophors—instruments that could project surprisingly large simultaneously televised images onto these large screens. We projected actions recorded at that very moment by cameras situated in *a*) two studios far from the theatre, *b*) on a Boston street in front of the theatre, *c*) in the audience, and *d*) on stage. In one of the studios we shot texts, photographs, and posters, and in the other, choruses and extras; in the audience, the spectators, and on stage, the actors. This pictorial collage was given coherence and meaning in the television control booth, which determined the sequence of images filling the giant receiver screens on stage. This enormously complex setup enabled the choruses in the studios to sing in response to the baton of the conductor seen on the monitor, who was in fact a live conductor conducting the orchestra in the theatre!

The chief significance of the system was to draw the spectator unexpectedly and very intensely into the play. A black singer sang a protest song; the camera in the audience panned the spectators and sent their image to the projection screens. People recognized themselves and were amused. At a certain point, however, we shifted the image from positive to negative; the audience on the screens suddenly appeared populated by blacks. Some spectators were indignant, and we again recorded their protest and projected it onto the screens. At one point we threw up the image of a live protest taking place in front of the theatre. The subject of intolerance dealt with in the opera, and the intolerance in the live context in which we presented it, were suddenly confronted. What was fiction and what was truth? In its total composition, this experiment has not been superceded, as far as I know.

It was also an example of how new technologies, new expressive resources, emerge. When a Renaissance artist sculpted a statue, perhaps an equestrian statue, he did it one way with sandstone, another way with marble. He couldn't achieve the postures and movements with marble that he could with bronze. He had to be in command of his material. If I'm going to use television technology, I have to become as familiar with it as with sandstone or marble.

Zimmermann. The Soldiers, *Staatsoper Munich, 1969. Dir: Václav Kašlík.*

Television, as complex as it may be, is simply another material. My thorough familiarity will lead to control and perhaps mastery. At all costs, I must not allow the material to control me. Needless to say, no one can understand everything. He must, however, know enough to communicate with the specialists who do. The designer may need to convince the specialist not to insist on certain constant technical parameters, because theatre can sometimes take advantage of even outright technical or material inconsistencies and transform them into quality results.

I worked on Zimmermann's *The Soldiers* for the first time in Munich in 1969, with Kašlík. The production was based on the use of multiple projection screens and film. *The Soldiers,* both in subject matter and music, is a classically dissonant work about a girl who dreams of a beautiful life but ends as a prostitute servicing army barracks. In 1976 I returned to *The Soldiers* with Götz Friedrich in Hamburg. This time I worked with purely theatrical means. Nine simultaneous scenes in three three-level constructions made use of the huge elevator lifts in the Hamburg State Opera. The vertical movement of these constructions, which had no walls, resulted in confrontations and compositions which helped to create the atmosphere of normal space and time. Concurrent with the story of an unhappy girl in bygone days was an ever-relevant indictment of a world that not only has soldiers but, more important, requires them.

On one of the stages, a group of naked recruits reluctantly entered a machine for producing military fabrics; on another they emerged uniformed, now snappily, already soldiers. On another of the stages, higher up, officers and ladies strolled about, while down below soldiers fell like little figures in a shooting gallery, and crosses were raised. It became an endless charade. The production had a distinctly anti-war character, while both of its thematic levels merged in an unforced way and strengthened each other. It was some of the most exciting work I've ever done.

In 1981 Götz Friedrich and I worked on a film version of the Hofmannsthal-Strauss *Elektra* for European television channels. Friedrich's basic concept was "revenge without absolution." He portrayed Elektra, who waits in vain for a liberator and avenger, as a prisoner of her own psyche. Orestes avenges his father's murder by murdering his mother and liberating Argos from the tyrant Aegisthus; but faced with the misery of Elektra, who is driven mad by her suffering, he has the doors and windows of the palace sealed. The liberator no longer needs her. Instead, he joins

Zimmermann. The Soldiers. Staatsoper, Hamburg, 1977. Dir: Götz Friedrich.

studio. I built into this space the ruins of the Labyrinth, the world in which Elektra gropes her way, where she has visions of her murdered father, and where she is observed by Clytemnestra from the window of a luxurious modern palace. Clytemnestra, while distanced from the actual site of the murder, cannot escape the deed. The smooth walls of the palace stream with blood. Film enabled us to place both environments in constant proximity, confronting each other to shocking dramatic effect. The essentially blue-gray, monochromatic decorations and costumes created a special tension with the red elements in the scene. In the very first scene, the slave girls scrub the blood-stained ground of the Labyrinth; Agamemnon's face has a red stain when it appears to Elektra; all of Elektra's hallucinations are intensely red. And the entire film takes place in the rain, yet it cannot wash away the spilled blood.

those in power as he begins to burden his conscience with new guilts. *Elektra* is left to die.

The operatic component was provided by Karl Böhm with the Vienna Philharmonic and singers, who had performed the work throughout the world. The singers became the chief actors of our film.

We converted an old locomotive factory into our film

I first met Richard Wagner during our production in Prague of *The Flying Dutchman* in 1959. Naturally I was aware of the dramatic power of his music. I grew, however, to appreciate the enormous challenge Wagner's work poses

Zimmermann. The Soldiers. Staatsoper, Hamburg, 1977. Dir: Götz Friedrich.

Wagner. Tristan and Isolde. *Bayreuth,. 1974. Dir: A. Everding.*

and yet transcendentally lasting love of the fated couple. While embracing its absolute ideal nature, I would also have to acknowledge its palpably sensuous character. I chose light as the sole means to achieve this effect. The shifting character of light enveloped the shimmering environment of the entire story. The scenography of the final scene, for example, in which Tristan waits for Isolde under a tree, was based on thin, densely clustered vertical cords. A mere change in the temperature of the colors projected onto the cords reconfigured the entire space. Tristan and Isolde were suddenly like sunspots, until at the end they became a part of the sun itself.

I also worked with Everding on the 1968 production of Carl Orff's *Prometheus* in Munich. I'm very fond of Orff's compositions, and the drama of Prometheus never ceases to excite me. I extended the forestage over the orchestra pit, and wedged a large piston-like block into a broad flight of stairs which rose up from the orchestra pit. The chorus appeared on stage during the initial blackout, as did Prometheus who remained fastened to the slightly inclined, oxidized but shining copper face of the block for the entire performance—a symbol of human greatness as well as impotence. We projected a larger than life image of Prometheus televised simultaneously onto the surface of the block to which the live Prometheus was pinioned. Toward

Wagner. The Flying Dutchman. *Bayreuth Festspiele, 1969. Dir: A. Everding*

to his collaborators as they extend themselves to match his music's effect.

But the degree of this challenge only became fully apparent later in Bayreuth, where I was invited by director August Everding in 1969 to work on *The Flying Dutchman* and then in 1974 on *Tristan and Isolde*. I wish that everyone could have the experience of encountering the best Wagnerian interpreters in the unique atmosphere of a Bayreuth performance! The very fact that people return to Bayreuth each year from all over the world to experience again and again this supreme peak of operatic creation evokes an atmosphere not unlike that which the Greeks associated with Olympus and Wagner with Valhalla.

We interpreted *The Flying Dutchman* as an authentic old ballad with an accent on its tragic-dramatic aspects, primarily conveyed by the choruses until the final monumental scene of Senta with the Dutchman.

For *Tristan and Isolde*, I sought to capture the unhappy

the end of the opera I illuminated this reflective surface with the light from fifty low-voltage spotlights which were placed on the edge of the loges. The reflection was so blinding that the spectators thought that the block was burning. The effect lasted for three seconds, and when the spectators could see clearly again, Prometheus had disappeared. He had been consumed by fire.

In 1972, Götz Friedrich invited me to work with him on the forthcoming production of Wagner's *Ring* for London's Royal Opera House at Covent Garden. This was the opportunity for which every scenographer longs all his life. The *Ring* was entirely unknown territory for both of us. The more we became involved in it, the more deeply we were drawn into the rich fabric of its images and associations. The *Ring* is as mythically powerful as *The Odyssey*, an epic of humanity's eternal struggle for power.

Much of our initial time was consumed by discarding ideas. Together, we finally saw the *Ring* as a vital cross-section carved from the history of planet Earth.

The setting became kinetic, without traditional decor. As usual, we progressed from the complex to the basic and finished with a truly simple idea which was prompted by the stage at Covent Garden itself. The stage on which a production evolves is the key to its understanding, which explains why I object to having plays transferred from one theatre to another. I wanted to interface the production with everything that Covent Garden had at its disposal. For example, I discovered that the stage had a trap area three and a half meters deep, in which it was possible to make an eleven by thirteen meter hole. I became intimately familiar with the trap area because I fell into it one day and lay unconscious at its bottom for a few moments. The problem of the waters of the Rhine was solved as a result. Reflecting the trap area on a large mirrored surface meant that the Rhinemaidens would not have to be seen directly. I suddenly had an auxiliary space, the kind that conjurors have for their magic.

The metaphoric witnessing of the birth of a *teatro mundi* whenever we are in a theatre was expressed by a special platform on which both the chorus and soloists could move

Photo: Group Three

Wagner. A technical photo of the Platform for the Ring cycle at the Royal Opera, London, 1974-1976. The mirrored undersurface reflected action in the trap area below stage level.

Wagner. Siegfried. Royal Opera, London. 1975 Dir: Götz Friedrich.

Photo: Jaromir Svoboda

freely. The telescopic column which supported the platform was capable of lifting it; a bearing within it enabled it to rotate. Four other smaller telescopic columns tilted it, and all these movements could occur simultaneously. At the same time, the boards covering the top surface of the platform had the ability, whenever the platform tilted beyond an angle of fifteen degrees, to change into stairs that angled in proportion to the tilt of the platform. The undersurface of the platform was covered with a perfect mirror surface, and this reflected whatever happened below the level of the stage. In short, we had in our hands a highly accomplished, flexible space and also an instrument for the entire *Ring*.

When the audience entered the theatre, they saw no curtain, but a banal, well-worn stage with black, rather old and dirty velvet draperies. The lights went out with the entrance of the conductor. The first few measures of the overture were heard in absolute darkness. When the lights finally came up on the stage floor, the platform began to emerge from its depths, as if its boards were a world in the process of being born. The platform rotated swiftly, like a model of the Ptolemaic view of the world. Then a very intense five centimeter point of light created by a red laser appeared on the cyclorama. Its fragmented granulation was the product of a special optical system which created kinetic laser graphics enriched by other colors, green and blue. The platform slowly began to stop rotating and inclined slightly.

Flecks of light on the platform revealed a new stage, a new world, a new reality, on which we played the *Ring* with all the resources of theatre past and present. We made use of dragons and snakes, but we also made use of computers. Indeed, it was only because the hydraulics were controlled by a computer that the movements of the platform could be continuous; its smooth motion from one position to another allowed the actors to stay on it. It was an instrument that enabled us to play all four operas with one fundamental scenography. We simply used other, equivalent resources for further configurations of space.

One of the marvelous resources was the projection of fire onto the platform. In *Siegfried* we covered the platform with ridges of extended metal, painted metalic silver on one side and matte black on the other; the metal was laid on a bed of black felt. The resulting surface provided great traction, and it was possible to move on it up to an inclination of thirty degrees. The platform, tilted toward the spectator, with the

through hanging vines. We used forced air to create a breeze that swayed the vines, creating new space on one side and then the other. This plastic material has a very good mechanical "memory" and quickly returns to its original position after every movement—which also helped me to solve the scene of Siegfried and the bear. We had a very inadequate bear, as we usually do at home in *The Bartered Bride*, but thanks to our "forest" the spectator didn't see him at all. Yet his presence was very effectively suggested, theatrically.

The first part of the *Ring, Das Rheingold*, should, we

Wagner Das Rheingold. *Royal Opera, London, 1974. Dir: Götz Friedrech.*

silvery surfaces of extended metal at the same angle, accepted unusually intense frontal projections. The opposite surfaces of the metal swallowed the upstage contralight and prevented the creation of undesirable parasitic light. It looked as though the entire platform was actually on fire. Siegfried moved about freely on its surface. The projection covered him as well as his costume; he seemed to be moving through flames.

What to do with the forest? Finally, I cut a thin, very pliant plastic material into strips, which I hung above the platform so thickly that the strips actually created a yielding mass through which an actor had to force himself as if

decided, have a mysterious character. The daughters of the Rhine emerged from the depths of the waters; and from the depths of the earth emerged Alberich, guardian of the gold, and capable of provoking the destruction of the world. On the upper surface of the platform, appeared Wotan, first among the equal demigods who stole the ring. At that moment the platform changed into a staircase, and the path to Valhalla, the path to Olympus, was open.

The second part, *Die Walküre*, was presented as a critique of the conflict between the world and human character. The platform, covered with a red cloth, became the blood-soaked earth. Wotan stood against the

Wagner. Götterdämmerung. *Royal Opera, London, 1976. Dir: Götz Friedrich.*

background of a black cyclorama in a marshall's cloak, with all the outward signs of his power, but isolated and terrified with fright before Alberich. Siegmund is his last hope, a "free man," who, like an outlaw, flees from the establishment "order," embodied in Hundig. After the

battle with Hundig, Siegmund's body lay at the edge of the stage, his head hanging over the orchestra pit. Hundig's force buried the hopes of Wotan as well. After abandoning Brunnhilde to her fate on the burning shield, Wotan himself departs into the depths of the stage like a tired, worn out commander.

Siegfried was our "black" fable. In the forest of vines lay Mime's foundry, equipped like a perfect workshop of some forgotten inventor. Siegfried goes into battle neither for power, nor gold, nor the ring, but to seek his lost identity. The fight with the dragon oscillated between a fight and persiflage; it was an excellently conceived pantomimic scene. But Siegfried ultimately gazed into the face of death. And then a spark of hope. Siegried passed through fire, and Brunnhilde, like Sleeping Beauty, awakened. Two people met, two people for whom gold, the ring, and power meant absolutely nothing; two people who simply love each other. This scene was illuminated by an almost clinically hard light to indicate that

Wagner. Die Walküre. *Royal Opera, London, 1974. Dir: Götz Friedrich.*

Wagner. Das Rheingold. *Grand Theatre, Geneva, 1975. Dir: J. C. Riber. The basic scenographic image for the Geneva* Ring *was an oval-shaped "ring" form in several layers, each of which had its own lighting complement. The oval was an integral entity only in* Rheingold*; in the subsequent operas it was fractured, and rejoined only at the end of* Götterdämmerung.

Siegfried's path was not yet finished. The realm of the Gibichungs still awaited him.

Götterdämmerung was a world transformed into a surgical operating room. It was created by large, transparent, suspended panels with thousands of optically reductive fresnel lenses with a focal length of minus thirty centimeters and a diameter of thirty-five centimeters. Each lens took in the audience space with its spectators. Into this system were also placed three lenses with a square format seven millimeters thick and a focal length of plus 1.60 meters which, on the contrary, magnified the performers. When Siegfried stepped into this space, he grew into a larger than life hero. As soon as he stepped out of this space, he became a slight man. It wasn't necessary for him to drink a bewitched potion. They simply "normalized-equalized" him according to their measure without his even being aware of it.

At Siegfried's death, three antique columns stood on stage, hiding the murderers, who crept away after their deed. The dead Siegfried, in a white costume, rested on a silvery surface. For the full ten minutes of the celebrated funeral march, the light falling on him intensified. And then suddenly the world, as if shaken by these events, moved. The lens descended, the columns lifted out, the one movement

blending with the other; the stage had changed without anyone being aware of it. And a lifeless Siegfried reposed at Brunnhilde's feet. We presented *Götterdämmerung* as an image of hell, an image of the end of humanity. This was a science fiction treatment of the world of the Gibichungs, which we as yet only naively imagine, but which perhaps already exists. Then everything was extinguished in flames, illuminating Valhalla for the last time. A man stepped on stage, a kind of pilgrim, and stood stark still gazing into the flames. Alberich, victor and vanquished, alone survives. The aggressive antagonism of the world had been interrupted. But not broken. The stage remained empty as if waiting for the beginning of a further play, a further world.

The first part of our London *Ring, Das Rheingold,* was presented in 1974. In that same year we also presented *Die Walküre; Siegfried* had its premiere in 1975 and *Götterdämmerung* in 1976. It had been an enormous, exhausting, but wonderful endeavor. An extremely difficult artistic problem will not destroy but on the contrary arouse and stimulate an artist, if there is a union of creative forces. This became evident during that same period as I collaborated on another *Ring* in Geneva, with director Jean Claude Riber.[2] It was an entirely different *Ring,* this time purely a fable, something like Jiří Trnka's *Midsummer Night's Dream.*

Opposite: Mozart. Idomeneo. *National Arts Center, Ottawa, 1981. Dir: Václav Kašlik Photo: Josef Svoboda*

ARTISTIC, COLLABORATION ABROAD

My early work abroad remains firmly in my memory as a great adventure, a period of eager searching and elation at suddenly discovered possibilities. Yet it didn't begin until after the 1958 world exhibition in Brussels, when I was almost forty years old. That sensation of life's youthful beginnings, as if they were a preparation for real life somewhere in the future, clearly derived from the conditions in which I was working.

At home I had twelve to fourteen productions each season. At the same time I headed the entire complex of workshops at the National Theatre. In the early years, when I'd leave Prague for a consultation or for rehearsals, my wife often accompanied me in our car and then waited for me in the front of the theatre. As soon as I was finished we raced home to Prague to be back at rehearsals or in the workshops by morning. So it went from September to June.

It was a time of unbroken tension and truly exhausting work. I confused days with nights, and even fainted from fatigue at my drawing table. But there was nothing to be done: I had to pursue the path I had begun at home. But I wanted to succeed in the larger world as well. Until 1958, however, when I was nearly forty, I knew the world only from literature. I was just beginning to learn how to swim in it without a lifeguard—and come to an understanding with it.

Success opened up new prospects. But there were also disquieting pressures: I was always expected to come up with something new and improved. I worked as if possessed; the greater the obstacles, the more intense were my efforts. The years flew by quickly. Yet as I look back it seems that there must have been far many more years than the calendar recorded, probably because they were so richly charged with varied experiences.

During my working travels in those days, I seldom saw more than the neighborhood around a theatre. I didn't know anyone abroad, either; my severely limited time was spent at rehearsals. As a result, I was all the more dependent on foreign colleagues and collaborators, some of whom played a particularly important part in my life.

My contact with the world beyond our borders began with my work on a few productions with foreign directors in Prague. The first foreign director to choose me was Jerzy Merunowicz of Poland, who was preparing a production of Stanislaw Moniuszko's *Halka* in the Smetana Theatre in Prague in 1951. Then the Soviet artists: Nikolai Dombrovski, who was working on Mussorgsky's *Boris Godunov* in Prague's National Theatre in 1954, and, in 1957, Gregorij Tovstonogov for Vishnevsky's *An Optimistic Tragedy*, also in the National Theatre. This third collaboration, as a result of my subsequent residencies in Leningrad and Moscow, turned into a sincere long-distance friendship.

Through Tovstonogov I became acquainted with the Russian classical and avant-garde theatre I had only imagined before. A sharp analyst with inexhaustible invention and a passionate desire for harmony, he brought to *An Optimistic Tragedy* an atmosphere of unremitting and yet creative discipline. It was an atmosphere undervalued by us, but unique artistic work never emerges without it. Twenty-five years later Tovstonogov's version of Tolstoy's story *Cholstomer* here in Prague testified that this patriarch of Soviet theatre hadn't aged and hadn't stopped taking the measure of everything he knew as if confronting it for the first time.[1]

My first invitation to work abroad came in 1958 from the theatre at Novosibirsk, from a group of young artists who had ideas considered unconventional for that time.[2] I already knew some of these people from 1954, when I was preparing an exhibit of my work in Moscow. Now I was to work on Janáček's *Jenufa* with director L. Michailov. Off I flew to Novosibirsk without any sort of information about the staging space or the director's intentions. But I had one fact straight: I would have a mere two weeks to conceive,

Berlioz. Les Troyens. *Grand Theatre, Geneva, 1974. Dir: J.C. Riber.*

draw, and build everything. Another fact intervened: I had an attack of pleurisy just before departure and felt awful. But the trip could not be postponed.

I flew on one of the first Soviet jetliners, a Tupolev. A four hour delay caused me to miss my connection in Moscow. It shouldn't be hard to imagine the efforts and complications I encountered in working my way to the commander of the Russian airfield to explain my situation! And I can't believe there would be many commanders anywhere in the world who would listen sympathetically to the urgent pleas of a set designer *en route* to a production of *Jenufa*. To my amazement, he not only sympathized, but he put me on a light army airplane headed in the direction of Novosibirsk. In fact, the commander sent a young guide along with me—but that poor young woman became ill during the flight and I had to take care of *her*.

The flight was marvelous: I never dreamt I would have the chance to see the Urals at such close range. We had an intermediate stop in Sverdovsk and ate supper completely alone in a large dining room of the airport building among many fully prepared tables; nevertheless, they separated us, putting me as a guest in one corner of the room and the crew in another.

As we were approaching the Novosibirsk airport, I

Offenbach. Orpheus in the Underworld. *Operetta Theatre, Moscow, 1965. Dir: G. Ansimov.*

wished I could have gotten off directly onto the roof of the theatre in order to know what fate was awaiting me. I noticed a cluster of people with cameras on the airport tarmac, apparently awaiting some sort of delegation. I quickly exchanged farewells with the crew and dashed off to the airport arrival hall. But there I was instructed to return to the steps of the airplane—and this time, descend slowly—and smile for the cameras!

Soon we were making our way through the intimately familiar labyrinth of an old theatre's hallways to the stage. And there, had I not been ashamed to do so, I could have sunk to the ground in despair. This wasn't a stage but a drill field with a twenty-five meter wide proscenium opening. How in God's name was I to put Jenufa's small sitting room in here?

As usual, ingenuity and hard work won out. Conditions for the required marathon were unusually favorable. Everyone worked enthusiastically without regard to preconceived notions or schedules. In a week everything was done including technical drawings!

And we still managed to drive to the famed regional pine forests in a brand new Volga auto; in fact, I even saw a bear. Novosibirsk at that time reminded me very strongly of my boyhood notions of the building of San Francisco. The workers who drove to the local taverns here on flatbed trucks on Sundays from the nearby construction sites reminded me of conquering explorers of the unknown. On my return, I had a three-hour layover in Moscow. It was a beautiful sun-filled day, and a grove of Russian birch trees was already beginning to turn green at the airport. I lay down on the grass, the birch leaves murmured and, gazing into the sky, I felt part of an authentically Chekhovian world.

I worked with Michailov once more in 1961 in Moscow during the production of Eugen Suchoň's *Krutnava*. We hit another major snag: how to improvise contralights. We experimented fruitlessly with several makeshift rigs until it occurred to me that we might use the headlights of locomotives. There must have been a railroad depot nearby because they immediately brought in several model lamps from which we were able to contrive a suitable effect. I returned to Moscow again in 1965 for a production of Offenbach's *Orpheus in the Underworld* at the invitation of Gregory Ansimov, whom I knew well from his guest directing in the National Theatre in Prague.

My encounters with the Russian theatre were always special occasions. I have never failed to envy the total commitment from the administrative personnel down to the gatekeeper towards the all-consuming goal of opening night. Even the discipline at rehearsals was unusual by our standards. I witnessed a rehearsal of *Camille* when the train arrival scene was repeated perhaps fifty times. No one considered it odd. If a director needed anything, it was obtained—with no debates. The effort to do everything to assure the best possible performance was extraordinarily impressive.

At the same time I became aware how the

based on lighting. The play was A. B. Vallejo's work about Goya's *Dream of Reason*. For A. Gelman's *Feedback*, in 1977, I proposed a pyramid backed by a mirrored cyclorama, which meant ordering special German reflective, pliable plastic sheeting (folios). And that wasn't all. I wanted the folios to be joined in one huge surface without folds or wrinkles. I myself didn't know how it could be done but I insisted that a way be found. They sent me home for a few days, and when I returned, it had been done. Just how they managed to do it remained their secret,

Gelman. Feedback. *Moscow Art Theatre, 1977. Dir: Oleg Jefremov.*

Photo: Josef Svoboda

characteristically Russian feeling for theatre—they share it with the English—makes the creators of a production almost automatically and subconsciously modulate production components in order to achieve an optimal equipoise among them.

My last work in Moscow occurred at the Moscow Art Theatre with Oleg Jefremov. In 1973 I did my first "incorporeal" scenography in Moscow—i.e., scenography

but it must have involved a terrific amount of work. As I was impatiently waiting at home for them to call me back, I couldn't help recalling another foreign production that had haunted me for a long time, even in my sleep: Stravinsky's *The Firebird* in Copenhagen in 1972.

I can't count the times that I have found myself in a desperate situation because my completed and approved proposals were not built on time or to specifications by

Stravinsky. The Firebird. *Royal Theatre, Copenhagen, 1972. Chor: E. Holm.*

theatre workshops. Or the number of times I had to change an entire conception at the last moment to compensate for external inadequacies. But nothing could ever compare to the horror I felt in Copenhagen. On that occasion, I and I alone was the sole perpetrator of the problem.

The scenography was based on a projection relief surface of several vertical layers of triangular surfaces in random configurations, the optical effect of which was multiplied by an upstage, irregularly shaped mirror measuring 15 x 15 meters, inclined toward the triangular clusters at a precise angle. The structure of triangles was surrounded by twenty-one Pani projectors with colored slides measuring 18 x 18 cm. The entire effect was to suggest the crowns of trees and was based on the principle of additive lighting, which required three projectors to be aimed at every projection area on the stage. By changing the slides and the intensity of the lighting, we should have achieved a continual change of colors. But after we had carefully prepared everything and turned on the lights at the first lighting rehearsal—to my horror and contrary to all assumptions—the scene was predominantly white! By manipulating the intensity, we managed at best some weak, completely undramatic images. Not until then did I realize that the projectors needed masks to demarcate with far greater precision the cluster of projection surfaces on which light was to fall, or not fall at all—or from only one of each cluster of three projectors.

Everything grew dark before my eyes. I immediately conceived of the only possible solution, but at the same time I realized how hopelessly laborious and risky it might prove. But there was no other way out, unless I wanted to admit a fiasco, there and then.

It's possible, of course, to change a projector into a photographic apparatus. We put a shield over the lens, used photographic plates instead of slides, and step by step "photographed" and immediately developed one section after another until we had photographs of all the groupings of triangles assigned to each triad of projectors. On the basis of this elaborate mapping, I might be able (with the help of masks) to cover the stage area to yield a coloration similar to my original intention. Of course, no one knew. The method had never been assayed before. This guinea pig was bred at a very high cost. Our only way out was a gamble of criminal proportions. If the gamble paid off, the extraordinary expense might be justified. If not, my career would be back at the drawing board. We did all the necessary work in one night. When we turned on all the lighting units the next morning, the result was truly beautiful. The mirrored reflection of the firebird absolutely danced in the crowns of the trees. Without the absolute understanding of all those in the theatre, without their desire to rescue the production, it would have been completely impossible. During my work at home I often grow nostalgic about the working atmosphere of many theatres abroad and about the people who are proud to belong to them.

I began to work in Germany at practically the same time as I did in the Soviet Union, first in the Deutsches Theater in East Berlin. I was lucky even here. The theatre had an excellent and, in the true sense of the word, progressive leader, Wolfgang Heinz. Both directors with whom I worked, H.D. Meves and F. Solter (himself a noted actor), were young and fully involved in their work. We quickly agreed that scenography had to be an active component of a play. Even the expertise of the routine technical personnel in the theatre was exceptionally high. An uncompromising precision ruled here—and I received a postgraduate education in real theatrical craftsmanship on a level that I had once experienced in the Theatre of the Fifth of May.

In Germany, at the Komische Opera, I met a man who

Gombrowicz. Operetta. Schiller Theatre, Berlin, 1972. Dir: Ernst Schröder.

was as significant in my work abroad as were Radok and Kašlík at home—Götz Friedrich. Nowhere in the world is there a more dedicated director and interpreter of Janáček's operatic works than Götz Friedrich. He has revealed Janáček to the world.

We have done the opera *From the House of the Dead* together twice, first in Zurich in 1978, and then at the beginning of his era as intendant in the Deutsche Oper in Berlin in 1981. As before, Friedrich and I quickly found a common working concept. Blind railroad tracks, a road leading nowhere, prisoners transferring railroad ties from one side to the other, futile soul-killing toil, as if every one of the prisoners were transferring his own imprisonment from one side to the other. Suspended above them, an eagle beats his wings against the bars of a cage, a symbol of imprisoned freedom. When he is finally released, he falls dead to the ground, because freedom came too late.

Sometimes Götz Friedrich and I don't see each other for years. And then perhaps on a February day the phone rings and we arrange a working meeting for the second of April at eight in the evening here or there. We meet, precisely on the minute, as if we had parted the previous evening; we don't have to explain anything to each other, we understand each other with only a few words, and we both have the brief but nevertheless unbelievably intense feeling that we're starting at the beginning yet again, with a lot still facing us.

In Germany I also enjoyed fruitful collaborative work in non-musical theatre. After seeing Faust in Berlin one day under Ernst Schröder's direction, I knew it would be a real pleasure to work with this man. And so it was. From the very beginning he attracted me with his Renaissance perspective—he directs, paints, and is an excellent actor. There isn't a problem that doesn't attract him; the most fantastic of fantasies are a challenge to him. He's an acknowledged expert on Dürrenmatt and Beckett. We prepared three Gombrowicz plays together in Berlin (*The Wedding* 1968, *Yvone* 1970, and *Operetta* 1972), and Shakespeare's *Tempest* in Munich in 1976. We understood each other readily, for we both spoke the language of designers, and the work flowed easily.

Both meetings, with Friedrich as with Schröder, were encounters of separate generations; yet we shared one factor in common— the Second World War, a divided world, and an urgent need to interpret those experiences.

A very different type of meeting occurred with Gunther Rennert in Munich. He belongs among those countless intendants of opera theatres throughout the world who are capable of blending the traditions of classical opera with new interpretations and production techniques. I have never seen anyone prepare a more thorough and masterful *mise en scène*. With his deep knowledge and love of Mozart he chose for *The Magic Flute* (1970) a scenographer with a reputation for breaking traditions. We worked together very well; I had the feeling that in his person I was meeting living opera history. I also began to understand why, despite prophecies to the contrary, opera still remains vital for many people and carries on triumphantly from age to age.

I had a very similar experience with the intendant of the Paris Opera, Rolfe Lieberman. Right from the beginning, he had an appreciation of my plans for Verdi's *Otello* in 1976. He was as convinced as I that both the libretto and the music called for a certain grandness of spectacle. In his search for a director he found Terry Hands, then of the Old

Verdi. Otel o. *Paris Opera, 1976. Dir: Terry Hands.*

Shakespeare. Antony and Cleopatra. *Schiller Theatre, Berlin, 1969. Dir: Fritz Körtner.*

Vic, who immediately understood what we were after.

I saw the storm as the key to the whole work: a storm in nature with a parallel storm within man himself. It began in the darkness and lashed at the eight-meter–high walls of the fort, which ascended in a stepped fashion. Only when the lights came up fully was it clear that on these steps stood a mass of people with their backs to the wall, forming a living rampart. The entire performance was done without changing any scenery. Spatial changes were created by architectural elements and enriched by virtual fireworks of light from low-voltage instruments; a drama of space developed from principles of lighting.

The spontaneous understanding and cooperation of all the interpreters was remarkable. Placido Domingo, who sang Otello, wasn't bothered at all in the famous "handkerchief" scene by having to gaze down from a height of five meters while standing on a beam one-meter long without any guardrail. He did it because it was necessary for the scene to make its full impact. I always think of him whenever I meet opera singers who don't understand

that opera is also—and perhaps above all—theatre.

I had an entirely different but unusually valuable human experience in 1969 with director F. Körtner, a famous Strindberg authority, in the Schiller Theatre in Berlin. He invited me to design a production of Shakespeare's *Antony and Cleopatra*. The entire performance was to be conceived as a fresco. Having jointly arrived at this departure point, I prepared the scenography accordingly.

About three weeks before the technical rehearsals I paid an unexpected visit to the theatre, where I discovered that my scenography didn't suit the director at all. We simply weren't speaking the same language. We went to lunch together and there, after some understandable hesitation, I shared my realization with him. He concurred and then added that he had never had this sort of talk with a designer. Körtner and I parted as colleagues who respect the distinctive character of each other's work. I shall never regret our meeting. Quite the contrary.

If I were to live anywhere in Germany, I would certainly choose Franconia. Gray sandstone and old-fashioned houses with emblems alternate with nature that seems almost virginal. Nearby are venerable Bamberg, Bayreuth, and Nuremburg, and next door is Erlangen with one of the most modern research institutes. That entire region, and director August Everding along with it, grew close to my heart one afternoon in June when we drove out of Bayreuth and stopped at a spacious garden restaurant. We were practically the only ones there, virtually encompassed by wonderful red cherries. The light was low, a quiet calm filled the air, and as I remembered Čáslav and my uncle's garden, I felt extraordinarily content.

Although I have wished the very opposite, August Everding and I have missed each other more often than we have actually met. We worked together for the first time in Munich on Orff's *Prometheus* in 1968. In all of his

subsequent work, I sensed a provocative inner inventiveness together with obvious discipline. Naturally I was pleased when he asked me to work with him on *The Flying Dutchman* at Bayreuth the following year.

The theatre on the green hill is a place where Wagner's works are genuinely worshipped. This truly marvelous theatre has a perfect wooden orchestra pit which descends by steps beneath the stage floor. The conductor cannot be seen, but by the same token the orchestra enjoys fantastic acoustics. Simply everything here serves the works created by a man who unlike anyone before him or anyone after him understood how to stage musically dramatic audio-visual compositions. The entire town is totally devoted to the productions which support its economy and its spirit. The Wagner season is like a convention of a special sect led

Wagner. The Flying Dutchman. *Bayreuth Festspielhaus, 1969. Dir: August Everding.*

Wagner. Tristan and Isolde. Bayreuth, 1974. Dir: A. Everding.

Wagner. Tristan and Isolde. Bayreuth, 1974. Dir: A. Everding.

by Wagner's family. And thanks to artistic director Wolfgang Wagner, each of the invited artists is immediately admitted into the sect, receives his own workroom, and—as a sign of welcome—finds a bottle of excellent Franconian wine on the table.

Our *Flying Dutchman* was a widely acknowledged success. Everding was exceptionally effective in staging the crowd scenes, but above all he integrated the scenography into the production as an absolute dramatic necessity, no less vital than the music itself. Five more years intervened before we met again in 1974, once more in Bayreuth to prepare my favorite Wagner work, *Tristan and Isolde*. Lighting rehearsals were, thanks to the lighting personnel, rather stormy, but the director's strength of purpose guided us to a truly striking final effect when the entire stage space literally dissolved into intense white light.

I did one more production with Everding after that, Orff's *Antigone* for the Zurich Opera in 1983. Since that time we have greeted each other, visited each other, and sent each other Christmas greetings, but otherwise our paths have not crossed. I often miss the soul-satisfying activity that we shared together.

My friendship with Armand Delcampe, director, manager, and actor, developed into another relationship of mutual understanding, respect, and joyful work during each subsequent encounter. His company based at the Theatre of Louvain University often travels throughout Europe, with some of its premieres at the Odeon in Paris.

For Claudel's *L'Échange* in 1982, which was to be produced at the Odeon, I proposed a "space for pseudo-plastic projection." It is an entirely neutral space that acquires a certain form only with the aid of lighting technology. To this day I remain occupied with its seemingly inexhaustible potential. The space is created by four-millimeter gray cords vertically stretched from the stage floor to a height of seven meters. The distance between the individual cords is four centimeters. In terms of the ground plan, these cords are irregularly clustered in sections a meter wide to a depth of seven meters so that the entire system can be walked through. It is, in fact, like a dense forest of vertical cords.

In previous productions I had great difficulty masking the cords' attachment to the floor. In *L'Échange* the solution offered itself. Since the action takes place on a beach, I covered the stage floor with ground-up cork to a height of twenty centimeters. It created a perfect illusion of sand; offered a beautiful color; was, of course, very light; created no dust, and gave the actors new possibilities for movement and business. When I covered the space with projections I was able to create an impression of infinite depth. The only other objects on stage were a swing and a rock. Armand and I agreed that the rock had to be absolutely naturalistic and about two and a half meters large. But I couldn't manage to get the rock to look right; no

95

matter how I reworked and painted it, it wasn't "it." Armand insisted that it must be perfect.

The persistent request that all elements on stage be maximally authentic usually comes from director-actors who look upon any artificial feature as a shortcoming that can seriously harm an actor's performance. I was genuinely

tunnel was another platform in the form of a ship's deck. The tunnel could, in fact, be transformed into almost anything by projections.

During this production I realized once again how completely an actor can transform himself. The platform for the ship fell apart into two pieces during a battle scene and

Pirandello. Six Characters in Search of an Author. *Atelier Theatrale, Louvain, 1984. Dir: Armand Delcampe.*

Photo: Josef Svoboda

concerned and persuaded about the problem in the case of the all-important rock. One day as I was wandering through the cemetery of Pere Lachaise, not far from the rehearsal quarters, I saw my rock in all its beauty. I made a very careful drawing of it, had it constructed, and it lived happily ever after on our stage.

In 1984, we did another Claudel together, *Break of Noon*. To create our performance space I stretched a high quality cotton scrim across the proscenium opening, which measured three meters by five meters. We thoroughly dampened this transparent material and then pressed into it a circle of two and a half meters in diameter. In an hour we had a tunnel of transparent material, a cavity, a paraboloid. We removed the scrim from within the circle, so that one could actually move through it. The bottom of the tunnel rested on a black, and therefore invisible, platform which followed the curve of the tunnel so that one could walk in it without the spectators realizing how it was done. Within the

simulated a ruined structure. Under it was an opening about forty-five centimeters wide. Through this incredibly small gap Armand—an actor who is anything but small— squeezed himself night after night onto the stage. Nobody knew the physics of his predicament better than I did. I still don't know how he managed it. But, of course, it wasn't physics; it was the actor's art.

Armand Delcampe is a theatre artist, body and soul. He is among those directors who first master a text rationally, analyze and examine it in detail, and only then begin their own creative work. And once he makes a decision he sticks with it. It was in such an atmosphere that we prepared the 1984 production of Pirandello's *Six Characters in Search of an Author*. Armand saw the director in the text as intoxicated by technology and determined to present a spectacular "show."

For an acting area, I proposed a violet-gray semicircular cyclorama that curved down to form the stage floor with

small, very carefully prepared openings. For the opening "show" we used all the wonders of audio-visual technology and raucous music. Then there was a sudden blackout, ostensibly caused by a short circuit, or so the audience believed. In this blackout we heard the voice of the stage-door attendant announcing some visitors. At that moment the stage lit up. There stood the six figures. When they started to enact the Father's story, each was provided a follow spot that also functioned as a projector via a central opening cut out of its painted gelatin filter. In effect, this special projector/follow spot created a pointillistic image around each of the figures. Each actor carried his color with him, and when two approached each other the overlapping colored projections created complementary colors, and, of course, the actors were thereby transformed. Everything else the scene required emerged from the floor—even a pool with little waves and floating leaves; and a tree which existed only as a shadow on the pool's surface. This Pirandello belongs among the distinct minority of my productions that turned out exactly as I envisioned them.

As I have come to see it, the difference between the German and the English theatre is the following: if during a performance a character suddenly appears in the balcony or on the ceiling, Germans immediately want to know how it got there and why, whereas the English merely evaluate the effect of the figure being there at all.

I had very much the same experience in England as I had in Russia, allowing, of course, for differences of national temperament. The English theatre artists are possessed by the art, a special group in an otherwise calm nation. They debate furiously, but always with an absolute sense of respect and democratic feeling toward all attitudes and opinions. It's an entirely unforced, natural, and totally effective form of teamwork. As soon as one is invited, he receives the full confidence of the group, just as in Bayreuth. Everyone is present at all rehearsals. Here, even I learned to attend rehearsals that didn't concern me, only to look on and observe, and to regard every performance after the opening as an important event.

My first English director was John Dexter, a member of Olivier's team. We put on Ostrovsky's *The Storm* in 1966 at the National Theatre. As a director, Dexter reminded me somewhat of Alfred Radok. In his presence, I had the feeling that everything was possible: textual editing and adaptation, unusual approaches and interpretations. Yet a deep respect and willingness to serve the author remained. Three years later, in 1969, we prepared Verdi's *Sicilian Vespers* in Hamburg. We agreed that a classical opera of this type could only be done with broad strokes and on a grand scale, not hiding, but on the contrary, emphasizing its operatic nature. The production had a truly long life, moving from Hamburg to Paris, on to New York, London, and Amsterdam. With each new presentation the scenography and direction evolved in response to the new spatial possibilities within each theatre.

The basis of the scenography was kinetic stairs and contralighting. As I stated, my frequent use of stairs is a regular subject for complaint at home. I plead guilty. But until actors and singers can fly, stairs will remain an elegant means towards the creation of necessary space, with the added benefit of their resonating surfaces. The only question is how to take maximum advantage of them.

Mussorgsky. Boris Godunov. *Staatsoper, Hamburg, 1972. Dir: John Dexter. The three walls were formed by huge projection screens that curved in at the bottom to form the floor.*

The stairs in *Sicilian Vespers* extended across the entire stage. Built into them, two circular towers would turn, then disappear to reveal a space consisting entirely of stairs and interiors. The stairs moved together and apart parallel to the audience to create dramatic configurations. Dexter supplemented this scenographic movement very effectively with appropriate blocking. In Hamburg in 1972 we also did Janáček's opera *From The House of the Dead* and Mussorgsky's *Boris Godunov*, the latter without changes of scenery and with only one intermission.

Later, when Dexter became head of the Metropolitan Opera in New York, we tackled Smetana's *The Bartered Bride*. Many people, especially abroad, have stumbled with this operatic gem of ours. The worst variation occurs when Smetana's work, so full of life, is handled as if it were a

relic from a museum. Dexter animated every bit of the stage. The response was exactly as one has learned to expect: enthusiasm from people who regard theatre as a living organism, and disappointment from those who wish to be reminded of their past.

I liked Dexter, this eternal boy with a great power of fantasy and an equally great restlessness. He was an agitated spirit, who always created a stir around him and understandably got on my nerves now and then. But his restlessness and agitation were always productive and ultimately creative.[3]

My first scenography for the National Theatre at the Old Vic was Ostrovsky's *The Storm*, with Dexter, for which I received the London Critic's Award. Then, in 1967, came my impatiently awaited partnership with Olivier on Chekhov's *The Three Sisters*.

One day a simple telegram arrived: "I'd like to work with you. L. Olivier." I wired back: "I'll be right there." To know Laurence Olivier at close range and to work with him was one of the great opportunities of a lifetime. I first saw him in person in Leningrad, where we were both on tour. Even before that he, and his work, had always aroused in me a sense of genuine wonder and respect. But I also felt provoked by its challenging and seemingly unapproachable perfection.

Each Chekhov production, regardless of location or artists, has always provoked and challenged me to attempt to capture the elusive atmosphere that glows from a Chekhov text. The production emerged from discussions with Olivier around a circular white table on which we sketched, and from an open exchange of ideas. I found Sir Laurence surprisingly tolerant and ready to accept the proposals of his appointed collaborators. I proposed to create the scene from cords and from them an illusion of infinity. Olivier immediately accepted my plans without the slightest doubts. His request that I create a curtain of light on stage surprised me. It was just at the time when I was being criticized for my scenography as being oppressive to actors. I was accused of overshadowing them or forcing them to move in unaccustomed ways. Olivier laughed at my concern: "Don't worry about it. You see, we are very good actors here."

And yet we did clash on two occasions. The first occurred when Olivier wanted a vision of Moscow actually to appear in the last act. I was horrified at the idea, but he stubbornly insisted. Finally, to my surprise and naturally to my relief, his vision actually worked. It was he who retreated the second time. The entire production was cast in a silvery gray color; Olivier suddenly wanted me to add green. There was no way in the world that I could accept this instruction. For three days we did not speak to each other. Sylva Langova, our interpreter, was desperate. Finally we reconciled our differences and the silvery gray color was saved.[4]

In London's Covent Garden—in a theatre where I also felt extraordinarily good working with an experienced and ambitious collective, and where Götz Friedrich and I presented the entire Wagner *Ring*—I also met conductor George Szolti. Szolti belongs to an exceptional group of musical artists with whom I have worked. The conductors I have known include Leonard Bernstein (I enjoyed a fantastic collaboration with him during the work on Bizet's *Carmen* at the Metropolitan Opera when director Goran Gentele suddenly died), then Claudio Abbado, Nello Santi, Maurice Bernardi, Karl Bohm, Colin Davis, Carlos Kleiber, and Silvio Varvisio; and Zdeněk

Chekhov. The Three Sisters. *National Theatre, London, 1967. Dir: Laurence Olivier. A wide ran; impressionistic effects derived from lighting the layers of stretched cords from the front, rear, ar al*

Chalabala and Jaroslav Krombholc at home. These people place their masterful talents at the service of opera-theatre. On the one hand absolute rulers on the conductor's podium, on the other hand active partners with the singers, directors, and scenographers, these extremely valuable people have a natural sense of self strong enough not to require them to assert their egos when the occasion calls for service.

Many years ago, when I made my commitment to theatre, I certainly wasn't including either opera or ballet in my mission. In contrast to opera at the Theatre of the Fifth of May, ballet left me alone and I reciprocated. It was not until Jiří Němeček invited me to Pilsen with the welcome

Tchaikovsky. Swan Lake. *Teatro alla Scala, Milan, 1982. Chor: N. Beriozoff.*

Photo: Josef Svoboda

proviso that I could consider the stage floor as part of the scenographic space, that ballet began to interest me.

Entering any new discipline isn't easy or simple. I needed to deepen my musical education, which at that time was concentrated primarily on opera. I had to begin to understand the alphabet of dance, and—what was most difficult—I had to learn how to light dancers, because light must not be allowed to dazzle or blind them. In fact, that's why the older ballets used footlights—diffused light doesn't blind but in fact helps orient the dancers.

Then in 1958 I was forced to throw myself head first into a study of ballet because of Laterna Magika. I started to attend dance performances at home and abroad, even musicals, from necessity at first, until ballet truly captured me. At home I subsequently worked most often with Jiří Němeček, Václav Kašlík, and Peter Weigl.

For a touring production of *Swan Lake* to be done by Milan's La Scala in 1982, I set out to design the most economical, most easily understandable, and the most symbolic distillation of this perennially interpreted story, and all of it to be transportable in a trunk. I started with the premise that Nature, the Priestess, and the Son represent good; the Sorcerer, evil. I concentrated all the surroundings into one transparent cloth panorama. It was hung so as not to touch the floor and cut to form a contour silhouette of the sorcerer's castle—upside down with a single illuminated window as a reflection in the water. The panorama, suspended above the center of the stage, divided the space into two halves covered at the sides and rear with black velvet. The velvet in the back was replaced in one place by a black translucent folio onto which was rear projected a filmed image of the moon seemingly broken up by the waves of the lake. After the spell was broken, the entire panorama, which was very light, collapsed to the floor, like a butterfly, and covered all the swans. It was in fact a curtain. I also had to deal with the great problem of creases and folds on a cyclorama but solved it by sewing it together in such a way that the material stretched itself out by its own weight.

Photo: Josef Svoboda

Berlioz. Symphonie Fantastique. *Paris Opera, 1975. Chor: Roland Petit.*

Of course, the man who really brought me into ballet was Roland Petit. He was already a legend during the time I began to travel abroad. His name was associated with those of Pablo Picasso, Jean Cocteau, Jacques Prevert, Jean Marais, Boris Kochna (one of Diaghilev's last collaborators), and those of the most celebrated stars of dance. He had made his impact as a dancer and exceptional choreographer very early. "As it was with Diaghilev, an ensemble of painters, choreographers, and dancers has assembled itself today around Roland Petit. We greet the birth of this ensemble and are overjoyed to have it occur in France, which Diaghilev so loved," wrote Jean Cocteau in celebrating the birth of Petit's Les Ballets des Champs Elysee after the war. He became famous throughout the world with his ballet *Carmen*, in which he danced Don Jose and his wife-to-be Zizi Jeanmaire danced Carmen. Doors opened to him in England and America. He disbanded and organized new ensembles, and became fascinated with musicals and the latest expressive resources of dance. Finally, in 1972, after touring throughout the world, he and his ballet ensemble settled in Marseilles, where he leads the ensemble to this day and where he has been the host for guest performances by Nureyev, Baryshnikov, and Maja

Plisecka, some of whose numbers were choreographed by Petit himself.

We met for the first time in 1975 to prepare Berlioz's *Symphonie Fantastique* for the Paris opera. For the first time at close range I came to know a choreographer able to lead dancers into a collaborative effort with scenography. The scene that I proposed consisted of three panels on wheels—three transparent mirrors 5 x 7 meters each, stretched over a metal frame which also functioned as projection surfaces. My proposal was accepted and turned over to the workshops to be produced. According to my contract I was not due to arrive until late in the rehearsal process. When I finally did arrive, I discovered that absolutely nothing had been prepared. All of France seemed to be on strike.

I now had twelve hours to reconceive the scenography. With technical help from my friends in Germany, I welded together sheets of the pliable gray projection folio called "Studio," manufactured by Gerriets, to create a universal interior without any solid construction. It hung freely from several lines and could, if desired, collapse entirely. Its walls were rigged to form two-part French curtains. The ceiling as well as the walls would collapse or sway in the wind, which came from fans set in the floor. The scenography was done on time and the production was successful.

In 1979 Petit with his Marseilles Ensemble and the music of Weiner and Doucet presented *Parisiana*. I shaped, transformed, and filled the space solely with lighting. A year later, with Claudio Abbado, we prepared Bartok's *Miraculous Mandarin* for Milan's La Scala. And once again I was attracted by this choreographer's ability to deal with space, to transform paradoxical situations and surroundings in a moment, and at the same time to maintain a remarkable stylistic unity.

In 1985 we met again in Berlin for the dance adaptation of a novel by Heinrich Mann, *Professor Unrat*, with music by M. Constant. The production was called *Blue Angel*, from the familiar film adapted from this novel long ago. The critics were unanimous in celebrating Petit's abilities with large and differentiated dance numbers joined with pantomimes and their mutual integration. My setting, based on the silhouette of a town, in front of which all the separate scenes were created by selected three-dimensional pieces, made this integration possible. Petit himself danced Professor Unrat, and Natalia Garova was his partner.

I regard my collaboration with Roland Petit as one of the gifts that life has granted me. In 1986 at the Congress Hall in Paris we did *Puss in Boots* with Tchaikovsky's music. Later we prepared a ballet which deals with the fateful story of the great Russian dancer Anna Pavlova.

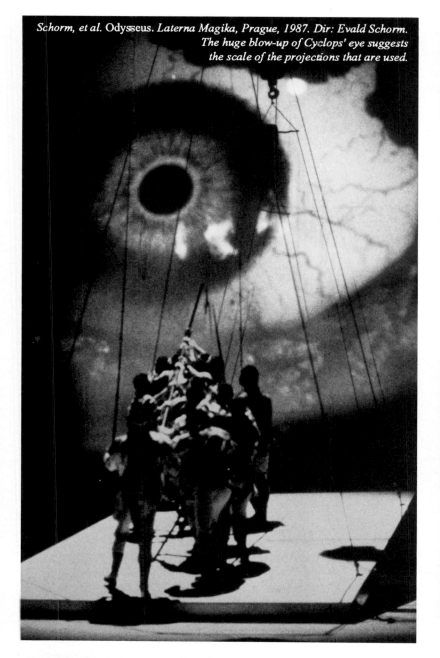

Schorm, et al. Odysseus. *Laterna Magika, Prague, 1987. Dir: Evald Schorm. The huge blow-up of Cyclops' eye suggests the scale of the projections that are used.*

Verdi. Nabucco. *The production was staged outdoors in a stadium in Zurich, 1986.Dir: J. Dexter.*

Verdi. Otello. *Grand Theatre, Geneva, 1980. Dir: J. C. Riber.*

Pirandello. Six Characters in Search of an Author. *Theatre Studio, Louvain, 1984. Dir: Armand Delcampe. The director chose to have the resident theatre company in the play working on a rock musical type of "show" before the entrance of the "six characters."*

Goethe. Faust. *I. Piccolo Teatro, Milan. 1989. Dir: Giorgio Strehler*

In every theatre that truly functions productively, you will invariably find one person who really makes it run—its impelling spirit or soul. Someone like Dana Pittichová, who for thirty-five years stood at the side of all the director-managers of our National Theatre. Her counterpart can be found in Geneva, in Zurich, in Oslo, in Louvain, in Munich, with Petit in Marseilles, and around the world. They love the theatre and continue to devote their entire lives to it. If they ever chanced to meet, they would see a surprising resemblance among themselves, and they would understand each other immediately. And their chiefs know what a treasure they have in them.

In the same way, all good theatres resemble each other in the modest scale of their administrative operations, with regard to the number of people involved as well as the physical facilities. The beautiful new theatre in Oslo has only a few offices, while every guest designer gets his own studio for the length of his stay. Wherever art really happens, administration is subordinated to bringing art to life.

The only way to do real theatre is with a team gathered around a distinctive creative personality, the way it was at home with K.H. Hilar, Jiří Frejka, E.F. Burian, or around the ripening personalities we had in the Theatre of the Fifth of May or in the National Theatre of the '60s. Otherwise it simply doesn't happen. Giorgio Strehler was such a figure whom I met practically at the end of my working career. We had known about each other for a long time, but our paths had never crossed until we were brought together by the work of all works—Goethe's *Faust*, in Milan's Piccolo Theatre. (I'm still in the middle of that project and therefore lack a necessary distance from it.[5])

For years I have recommended that the National Theatre have several rehearsal studios, with appropriate support systems, in addition to new workshops. Each new production would be given its own studio for the entire length of its preparation. A minimal production staff would assure the ongoing progress of rehearsals. A production could then develop before the eyes of its creators without distractions for the entire length of its creative rehearsal process. I feel sad when I encounter this "miracle" throughout the world wherever I go, but not at home. As if anyone could tell Strehler he must make definite decisions about scenery, costumes, and the overall appearance of a production a full year before his first rehearsals!

After all, it's only during experiment and rehearsal that ideas begin to acquire form, and new and unexpected connections or counterpoints begin to emerge. With Giorgio Strehler, I always experience anew the adventure of creativity, in which all possibilities remain open to the last moment.

Bartok. Miraculous Mandarin. *La Scala, Milan, 1980. Chor: R. Petit.*

Opposite: Rychman. Noricama. *Nuremberg, 1971. Dir: L. Rychman.*

EXHIBITION AS
WORLD OUTLOOK

Although I never thought I'd become involved with the scenographic problems of ballet—I was mistaken. And I never gave any thought at all to exhibition work—but I found myself doing that as well.

One day, I realized that large exhibitions can experiment with things that theatre can't afford to think about. At the same time I should add that we developed nothing new during our exhibition work that we hadn't already begun to experiment with in theatre. The problem was that we were not able to experiment on a large scale.

Like the Olympics, great world exhibitions ought to provide each host country with an opportunity for self-help as well as self-expression. Instead of designing pavilions that are frightfully expensive and usually worthless once the exhibition is over, international architects should compete to project the most ideal city plan for a certain section of the host city. And all the participating nations would contribute their outstanding products and creations. The result would

art, and our first entry into competition without knowing the strength of our opponents.

We were unusually lucky that those who prepared our exhibition understood that world exhibitions are first of all surveys of ideas, not buildings and objects, no matter how well made. What was at first glance a banal theme—one day in Czechoslovakia—was presented in our pavilion with such freshness, immediate effectiveness, and taste that it captivated the severest critics.

I participated in the exhibition as the interior designer of the cultural hall, as the creator of Polyekran (the director of its "Prague Musical Spring" program was Emil Radok), as a joint creator of Laterna Magika (together with director Alfred Radok), and as a designer of a separate section of the Czech Glass exhibit ("The Tradition of Czech Glass"), and of part of the Industrial Machinery exhibit ("Antenna Receiver").

While working on the design for the cultural hall I realized that an exhibition makes sense only when its own scenography is based on the idea of the exhibition as a whole, exactly as theatre scenography is based on the text

Radok, E. Polyekran; Prague Musical Spring. *Brussels Expo 58. Dir: Emil Radok.*

Photo: Miroslav Pflug

be both an exhibition and a living model of the contemporary world's achievements, understood by everyone, and of long-lasting, practical usefulness.

The world exposition in Brussels, so-called Expo 58, had special significance for Czech and Slovak culture. It was our first participation in a world exhibition after 1945, our first display of our sense of the historical evolution of our

of a play. Its "action" must bring the spectator or visitor to identify with it. This idea directly led to my first Polyekran and our Laterna Magika.

I submitted my first proposals for Polyekran and its program "Prague Musical Spring" in July 1957, and was officially assigned the work in October 1957. I wanted Alfred Radok to direct, but because of his schedule on the

Svoboda. Polyvision. *Montreal Expo 67. Dir: Josef Svoboda.*

Laterna Magika program he recommended his brother Emil. I arranged my initial technical consultations privately until, in December 1957, the construction and manufacture of Polyekran was taken over by the Research Institute of Sound, Pictorial, and Reproductional Technology in Prague.

The goal was to create space by means of projected images on a series of strategically positioned screens. It was exciting, feverish work and time limits put us under great pressure. Sometimes the technical conditions stimulated us to new ideas, at other times they restricted us, but ultimately we freed ourselves from traditional film formats and methods of classical cutting to create a polyphonic composition of multiple images and high-fidelity sound.

The "Prague Musical Spring" scenography provided the director with eight projection surfaces (squares and trapeziums) distributed in a black space. Though the viewers were situated fairly close to these surfaces they could nevertheless take them all in together. The intimate seating space was filled with stereophonic sound from a cluster of loudspeakers arranged to create the illusion that the entire space resounded. The projection surfaces were hit by alternating moving and static images from seven film projectors and eight slide projectors.

The technical design, which had been proposed by the Research Institute, was based on a kind of "memory" circuit that controlled all program functions, including the synchronization of music. In those days the construction of

such an "intelligent" instrument was extraordinarily difficult, and thanks are due to Miroslav Pflug for putting it all together and having it function perfectly.

The unbelievably short time we had at our disposal meant everything had to be definitive from the very beginning, music as well as film and spatial composition. It's a method against which a theatre person, who is used to the gradual evolution of a work, instinctively rebels, but there was no other way. Before our departure for Brussels we had only a few working rehearsals, and the first time we all saw the entire program was in Brussels itself a few days before the opening of the exhibit—when it was already too late to make any changes.

At home the prevailing opinion was that the whole scenographic system and indeed the program itself would be too demanding and exclusive for the average visitor to the exhibit. By pure accident, our first visitor was one of the Flemish watchmen at the exhibit, whose reaction was so favorable and authentic that we felt genuinely relieved. Once the exhibit opened officially and each performance was followed by enthusiastic applause—not a usual response to films—we began to relax. "Polyekran," which we subsequently named the new projection system, began its career in the world, and our many Expo experiences strengthened and enriched us for our future work.

In 1967, long after our Brussels success, I was invited to work on the World Exhibition in Montreal; specifically, I was to propose a design for one entire exhibit and to organize its large space. My response was an audio/visual complex I called Polyvision. It was made up of four systems, all stemming from the Brussels experience. The first consisted of projections onto cubes and prisms, as well as onto bodies created by rotating elements. All these bodies moved horizontally as well as vertically, and their movements (as well as the entire space) were heightened by mirrors inclined in various ways either toward or away from the viewer. I prepared the scenario and the direction for this

also prepared the scenario and the direction for this program, "The State of Textiles."

Finally, the fourth system was based on eighteen static circular surfaces, which created an unusual projection surface. The scenario and direction of this program, which dealt with atomic technology, was taken over by Jaroslav Beránek.

The entire exposition with its four systems created an entity, which a viewer could follow as a whole. That was as far as we were able to go with electronics based on a

Radok. Diapolyekran; The Birth of the World. Montreal Expo 67. Dir: Emil Radok.

program, "Symphony," myself.

The second system created a mosaic wall composed of 112 cubes, each of which was supplied with two slide projectors holding eighty slides each. Each cube was thereby capable of 160 changes. Individual cubes could move forward or backward either a half-meter or a meter, so that the maximal depth of the resulting relief surface added up to two meters. The goal of all this was to create pictorial units, but also to disintegrate the projection surface and to compose and estrange its relief profile in new ways. We called the system Diapolyekran. I asked Emil Radok to supply the scenario and the directorial program for this exhibit, "The Birth of the World."

The third system filled a given space with three stringed rectangles which moved and overlapped in such a way as to make a projection surface that acquired varying densities. I

"carousel" technology. Then computers came along and, based on our principle, began to create miracles on running tape. Today's Jumbo system has demonstrated how much modern technology can do based on ideas that originated with us over thirty years ago.

In 1971, for an exhibit devoted to the memory of Albrecht Dürer in Nuremberg, I prepared another audio-visual production called "Noricama" (because it was commissioned for Nuremberg). It was the last exhibit in which we were able to make some minor technological progress. "Noricama" consisted of a projection surface in the form of cinemascope, vertically divided into five screens. Each screen could retreat to a depth of five meters, but also could stop at any point at will and thereby create the most varied kind of scenic space. Each of these five surfaces was assigned a film projector that moved together with the surface. In addition, the space in front of the entire large surface was given over to a system of slide projections on *other* projection surfaces of various formats, which appeared and disappeared as needed.

The exhibit was conceived as a dramatic work in its own fashion. Our program, the scenarist and director of which was Ladislav Rychman, presented an interesting view of Dürer but also of German history through the apocalypse of the Second World War and up to the present. It attracted viewers to Nuremberg castle for ten years.

In 1973 I designed the interior of the American pavilion for an exposition in Montreal, the theme of which was ecology. The pavilion—a huge glass sphere filled with

of their pavilions. I chose the theme "America Now, At This Moment." The foundation of the proposal was a mirrored cube, which reflected its surrounding area, while its six interior walls were covered by large-screen television monitors. Within the cube, viewers would be on a transparent platform from which they could see all the inner walls, even the one beneath them. The platform would be smaller than the walls of the cube and would be suspended within them. By means of mobile TV reporting vans distributed around the United States, a series of shots would be made available to the director, who would arrange them into a dramatic sequence, and commentators who would not know which pictures were awaiting them would be forced

Rychman. Noricama. *Nuremberg, 1971. Dir: L. Rychman.*

daylight—had stood there since the 1967 exposition. After many years I was again faced with the same problem that I had in Novosibirsk. What to do with such a great (and now sun-filled) space? For a long time I wasn't able to come up with anything, until the theme of this exhibit itself—"Man and His Environment"—led me to a design concept. After all, we live in a world filled with clean and unclean molecules.

I filled the entire pavilion with black and white balloons of lightweight rubber with a diameter of approximately thirty centimeters. The white ones were concurrently projection surfaces for films showing images of unspoiled nature. Once released in the huge sphere, the thousands of balloons attached themselves to the walls and thereby darkened the pavilion. The visitors had to make their way through these balloons, and the physical contact with the white "bountiful" ones and the black "polluted" molecules was extraordinarily suggestive; the entire pavilion gave the impression of some sort of molecular Altamira.

I took part in a number of subsequent exhibitions at home and abroad, but what lies closest to my heart are four projects that were and will remain my unfulfilled dreams. Two concern the World Exposition in Osaka in 1969.

The Americans invited me to submit a proposal for one

to react on the spot to everything that the spectators would see of American reality. The images were to be transmitted to Osaka by means of a television signal from a satellite. It could have been exciting theatre dealing with exciting reality, but controlling a satellite solely for Osaka was too costly in those days.

I actually had an idea for our own exhibit in Osaka but I never made it public.[1] Imagine a large field bordered by a slate wall and on it various writings, such as an invitation to the visitors to add their own greetings or invitations. And within these walls would be the garden of Bohemia— sculptured versions of our flora and fauna, everything we have that nourishes our natural surroundings. And, of course, a great wooden sculpture of a leaf-filled linden tree, hollowed out as it is in Jirásek's *The Lantern*. In one corner of the garden would be an entrance to a cavern like our Macocha or Dobšín, sculpted of Czech glass and supplemented with an audiovisual system. Visitors would be guided through the cavern by a hostess who would soon transform into a nymph, then into still another fairy tale figure to escort them through the world of Czech fables and legends.

The visitors would walk through a forest and arrive at a glade, where seated around a bonfire twelve moons alternate in their rule over nature. At the edge of the forest they would encounter a storybook lord: "See the lord riding from the forest, riding on a stallion, black prancing stallion, hooves ringing gaily, riding all alone." Along a river, from which mute fish would emerge with strange rings dug from the depths of the river bottom, a boat would drift by. The visitors would step into it and drift through the realm of water spirits, bordered by the bent heads of willows and full of dozing spirits. Then they would go on foot again through narrow paths around village graveyards, until on a slight hill between the wooded portions appeared "the little church with the low tower." They would hear the song of shepherds and before them Mount Blaník would slowly open,

lower part. "Please come back whenever you have an idea of what to do with the space," the Archbishop said. To this day, I haven't had an idea, and I would hardly venture to suggest anything. The problem is that I've been smitten forever by Michelangelo's "Birth of the World" in the copula of the Sistine Chapel in Rome; I simply wouldn't dare to tackle a similar theme.

One other unrealized project haunts me most of all: a theatre I have never built, although twice I came fairly close. During the opening of an exhibit of my work in Paris in the mid-1960s, the French Minister at the time, Andre Malraux, suggested that I prepare a project for a theatre building for Paris-East. It was, for me, a fantastic

Rychman. Noricama. *Nuremberg, 1971. Dir: L. Rychman.*

revealing toward the rear of its depths a treasure chest full of jewels. They would enter, the mountain would close behind them, the treasure chest would disappear, and they would be left to face two exits. One would lead them directly back to the beginning along a wide stairway; the other along a wooden circular staircase into the interior of the linden tree. Awaiting them there would be a true treasure, Erben's verses:

You who have ears to hear
Why block them with your thumbs?
And you who have reason from on high,
Why trample it under your feet?

Above ground, the garden of the Czechs, and below the hidden, ancient secret of their soul—that was and remains my dream for an exhibition that never was.

In 1973 Miroslav Pflug and I were surprised by an invitation to meet with the archbishop of the Cathedral of St. Joseph in Montreal; he wished to offer us a special project.

The copula of his cathedral has two layers: from inside you see only the lower layer and from outside only the upper. Between the two is hidden an enormous space, reached only by elevator. Viewers would probably move inside it on a double spiral resting on the surface of the

offer, because the site and disposition of the area would have made it possible to build a truly extraordinary transformable and functional theatre, one that would have satisfied all contemporary parameters. I worked on the project two and a half years with the director of the Theatre National d'Est Parisien, Guy Retore, and completed it successfully. Unfortunately, however, the end of the 1960s brought the student uprisings and strikes, changes in the government, and our project was never realized.

A similar fate awaited a project for a separate theatre building for Laterna Magika, situated above the Spálená Street exit of track B of the Prague underground. Here, too, the site and disposition of the area were optimal and the budget for the construction unbelievably low, because we would have been able to use the Metro as a foundation. It was a project for a consistently variable theatre including its audience area, which was always my ideal, as I describe elsewhere. The project will not be accomplished in my lifetime, and Prague will still lack a truly modern theatre. Too many resources were used during the reconstruction of the National Theatre and the building of the New Scene. Even if I were to live and work for many more years, the fact that I haven't built one single theatre in my career will remain a great misfortune for me to the end of my days.

Opposite: Máša. Vivisection. *Laterna Magika, Prague, 1987. Dir: Antonin Máša.*
Scenography: Vladimír Soukenka. The lower panels rotated to reveal
an upstage area, and the small screen could be lifted out.
Photo: Vojtěch Pisařik, courtesy Laterna Magika

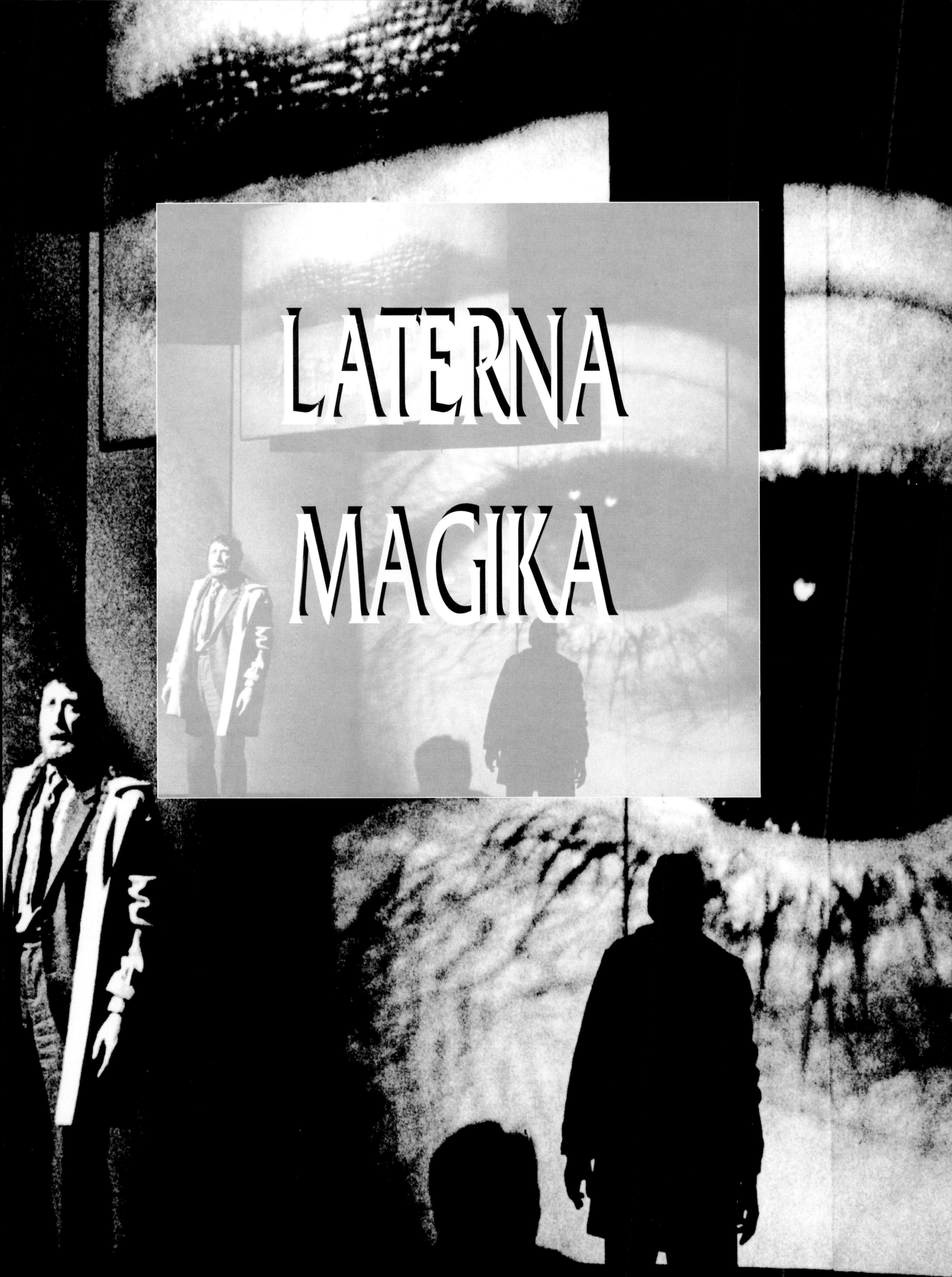
LATERNA
MAGIKA

In 1881 F. F. Šamberk wrote *The Eleventh Commandment* for the Provisional Theatre. For seventy years, the most varied professional and amateur theatres performed it throughout the country. The great character actor Jindřich Mošna played one of his celebrated roles in it for the National Theatre. In 1950 we decided to stage it in the State Film Theatre.

Alfred Radok and I had already done numerous productions together in the Theatre of the Fifth of May, where we had taken "new" approaches to old material. *The Eleventh Commandment* was a different matter. Radok adapted the three-act drama into a two-part vaudeville set circa 1910; the music and lyrics by Jiří Sternwald provided a subtitle—*The Eleventh Commandment, or Most Highly Esteemed Mr. Urban*. In its total style, the adaptation resembled slapstick farce. The filmed portion was drawn in part from magazines of the period, which featured, in addition to sensational reports of automobile and flying events, Emperor Franz Joseph himself. It was also composed of scenes shot in exteriors with the same actors who performed on stage. The chief characters were a foursome of friends who promise each other they'll never marry. This very successful production was, in fact, also the first performance of Laterna Magika, though we didn't know it at the time.

Seven years later we were faced with the question of how to publicize Czechoslovakia in the cultural hall of the 1958 World's Fair in Brussels. We decided to put together a brief, very special theatrical presentation. Our deliberations of many years about a polyphonic theatre became our point of departure. We would articulate the relations between actions on a screen and on the stage as neither mechanical nor illusionary, neither illustrational filmed projections (à la Piscator) nor a naturalistic illusion of reality. Film would remain film and the stage the stage; we would simply exploit the manner in which we joined the actions on stage with those on the screen.

Understandably, we were concerned whether the viewers would even be capable of perceiving several actions, images, or sounds at once. Would it be possible to join filmed action with stage action freely; would we be capable of using film cuts to influence the action on stage? Nor did we know the extent to which one could multiply the relations between the two media by means of various combinations of various projection surfaces. We knew that a mechanical joining of film and stage scene would offer a series of "gags" that might amuse a visitor. But could such "gags" be organized into a viable theatrical presentation?

As a designer I was faced with using a small stage space for the most disparate actions: the appearance of our mistress of ceremonies, for example, accompanied by her two filmed images. Into this same space I was also supposed to squeeze a small brass band and make room

for one male and three female dancers, a piano, as well as other properties. The guideline for every change required that the design relationships between the individual projection surfaces and the total space of the stage be maintained. At the same time I had to orchestrate all the mechanical movements on stage.

Our dramaturgical, directorial, and design plan presupposed that every individual component on the stage would have a number of functions, the multiplicity of

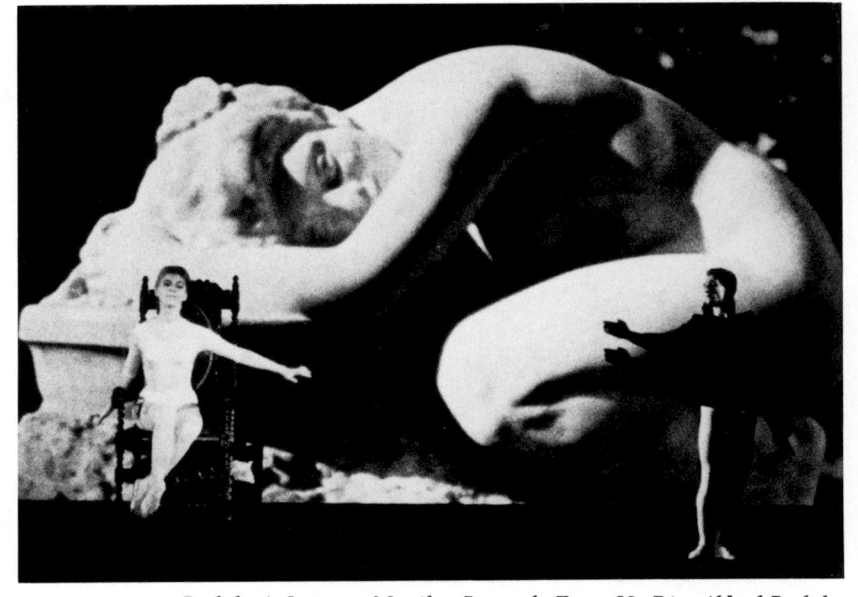

Radok, A. Laterna Magika. Brussels Expo 58. Dir: Alfred Radok.

which would help reinforce the rhythmic changes in the presentation. The entire project, which was joined by composer O.F. Korte and Miloš Forman as scenarist, was named Laterna Magika by Alfred Radok.

Our stage, lined with black velvet, with the floor covered by black felt, had a floor measuring 12 x 7 meters, and a height of 5.5 meters. The actual acting area measured 12 x 5 meters. The trap area, which measured 5.78 x 1.8 meters, could sink to a depth of 2.5 meters. It was situated immediately in front of the rear cinemascope projection surface, which was covered with black velvet curtains that opened and closed like a camera shutter. Because the curtain tracks were motorized, these curtains could be operated either individually or from all four sides at once.

The rear part of the scenography had a surface of 8.5 x 4.25 meters, containing two rotatable projection surfaces (one at each side measuring 1.7 x 4 meters), which disappeared from view when rotated 180 degrees. The remainder of the rear part was covered by black velvet. The rotatable projection surfaces and the rear projection surface were covered by a single projector with an anamorphic, cinemascopic lens.

The middle part of the scenography with a projection surface of 3.5 x 2.5 meters, had concealed doors and rose up from the trap area. Its entire surface could be covered by a single, classical format projector. The scenography's front projection surface measured 3.75 x 2.5 meters. It was lowered in and could also be covered by a classical format projector.

The projection booth was equipped with three film projectors (one of which could be tilted away from the projection axis) and a slide projector for slides 13 x 13 centimeters. The stage lighting was controlled by an ADB board for twenty circuits, handling up to twenty spotlights from 500 to 1000 watts. The sound was multi-channel stereophonic.

A performance of Laterna Magika, like every other theatrical performance, is a matter of sight and hearing,

performance and broke them down into mere individual numbers. And, on the contrary, we were convinced that if we observed certain guidelines we could achieve generally valid and noteworthy theatrical results.

Modern theatre begins when actors seriously relate to the actual characters of the drama, rather than simply to other actors on stage. Internally they connect to everything happening on stage, even to the props; externally, they must have an effect on the audience. Stanislavsky himself

Radok, A. Laterna Magika. Brussels Expo 58. Dir: Alfred Radok. The live performer and the screened images are mutually dependent; they function together simultaneously.

but in our case, of course, its composition was primarily created by linking and arranging the individual program segments. The overall form of this total system then evolved from the style of the presentation and its rhythmic treatment.

Debates on whether Laterna Magika is really theatre or not raged from its very beginning. We believed that Laterna Magika would cease being theatre if we interfered with the pattern of certain rhythmic changes in the

formulated this principle very precisely. Radok insisted that Laterna Magika, by making use of new resources, demonstrated to everyone's surprise that Stanislavsky's precepts weren't empty theory.

For instance, the "conference" scene from Laterna Magika's first program was conducted on stage by the Mistress of Ceremonies character. Her partners were two filmed images of herself. To bring them to life, she had to establish inner contact with them, just as the two filmed

Photo: Pavel Horník

Photo: Jaromír Svoboda

Three scenes from The Magical Circus

Schorm, et al. The Magical Circus. *Laterna Magika, Prague, 1977.*
Dir: Evald Schorm.

mistresses of ceremony had to react to each other as well as to the living representation on stage. In fact, we presented proof of Stanislavsky's principle of suggestion and autosuggestion.

The actress on stage and, in our case, the same actress on two screens, behaved as though all of them were actually present. The viewer in the audience was, of course, aware of a mistress of ceremony on stage as distinct from two others on the screens, but he unconsciously perceived all three as part of one dramatic action.

contrast and learned how effectively joined heterogeneous elements can create a unified style. This effective joining was not merely a matter of selecting the individual, heterogeneous elements, but determining, first, how to tie them together, then how to make them interact.

The rhythm of the presentation as a whole must unconditionally be created in advance precisely as a music score; that's the sine qua non of the Laterna Magika production process. It relates to everything—to content and form, to time and space—and reveals just how much the

Radok, A. Laterna Magika. Brussels Expo 58. Dir: Alfred Radok. One number from Laterna Magika. Five separately filmed and projected images of the live pianist on stage interact with each other and the performers on stage.

The question remained how to join entirely disparate materials into one resulting style. Our program was supposed to incorporate existing public relations films about contemporary factories, iron works, and the beauties of the Czech countryside. Radok used to say that when he began to think of Degas dancers in connection with contemporary film clips, he wasn't aware that he was actually moving toward the essence of Laterna Magika.

The result, called "Slovanic Dances," became part of the first program. In it we verified the possibilities of

creators of the presentation know or don't know. It's a purposeful orchestration of all the measurable changes and all the diverse components embraced within the scenic-dramatic space.

It was not by coincidence, then, that one whole segment of the second program, in 1959, was titled "rhythms." It turned out to be a practical demonstration of rhythm theories. Its filmed portion was composed of routine clips of sporting events, technology, and industry, as well as ballet exercises and calendar cover illustrations of well-

114

known castles and fortresses. These film clips were contrapuntally interrupted twice by a marble statue that circled the stage, functioning as a component of theatrical scenery.

The music had within it traces of the most varied musical sources, from actual human voices to large and small orchestras, to elements of modern dance, and back again to madrigals. Similarly, the choreography alternated passages from classical ballet, social dancing, acrobatics, and back again. It was precisely from the contrasts within this utterly heterogeneous material that a special dramatic tension resulted.

With film, music, choreography, and scenography, we always consciously used familiar, if not common, elements, and precisely by means of their individualized orchestration we achieved a new artistic reality, thus building on some of our earlier theatre work. We became aware that the emotional associations of the "familiar" can become a production component of our polyscenic stage creation, a component whose meaning transcends normal logic and deepens psychological perception.

The essence of film's artificial reality was also found to lie in the perception of simple signs and in the viewers' need to become accustomed to their patterning and significance and to learn how to look more deeply. The very style of the film seemingly enveloped the characters of the film with its own, further significance.

We also verified that as soon as the same psychological or logical actions—that is, aggregates of certain signs—are processed several times in the same manner, the manner itself begins to bear a further, distinct meaning.

After all, our affective memory, which draws from realities of daily life as well as from various non-objective or imagined realities, is capable of expanding their meaning to form patterns of affective association, which in a special way deepen and enrich those realities with added significance. This is a process which today's art may safely count on.

The second program of Laterna Magika also included a production of Bohuslav Martinů's musical work based on Miroslav Bureš's text *The Opening of the Wells*. Its filmed portion was expertly innovative (camera, Jaroslav Kučera), yet we confronted a critical problem: how to find an expressive stage embodiment for the film; our failure was a violation of the crucial principle that binds Laterna Magika to theatre. Even though this program was as successful as the first, and we discovered in it much that was new to us, it was clear that our new system could evolve only by means of a different approach, clear in theory but difficult in practice.

An obvious break in the evolution of Laterna Magika was its transfer from an experimental scene of the National Theatre to an experimental studio of Czechoslovakian State Film; still later, it was administered by the State Theatre Studio. I worked only once with Laterna Magika during this period, in 1962, on the *Tales of Hoffmann* program, directed by Václav Kašlík. We thus tackled an opera and tested a number of new approaches. The result was a success, but we became aware that questions about the relationship between the actor on stage and on the screen remained wide open. The stylistic purity of presentation was a problem yet to be solved. In short,

115

Radok, A. Laterna Magika. Brussels Expo 58. Dir: Alfred Radok.

even here Laterna Magika's crucial canons were insufficiently respected.

In the following years, Laterna Magika concentrated on long-term residencies abroad with programs made up of individual numbers altered or modified as needs arose. Individual gags were changed, but there was no evolution of either dramaturgical or production principles. Even the staffing of performers and creative teams was altered. Earlier, the great majority were members of the National Theatre, but now Laterna Magika assembled its own creative teams and even its own dance company. Unless faced with constantly fresh creative goals, every artistic body must of necessity decline in quality. This caveat applies especially to Laterna Magika, for which mere repetition is a mortal danger.

I have rarely vacillated as much before a decision as I did in 1973, when I was asked to become head of Laterna Magika and bring it back into the National Theatre. When I decided to meet the challenge I knew I was risking my professional reputation.

In the "transitional" period, as we in Laterna Magika used to call the years 1973-1977, we presented two programs—The Prague Carnival with director Václav Kašlík, and *The Lost Fairy Tale* with director Jaromil Jireš. *The Prague Carnival*, tales from Prague mythology, was in many respects an interesting work but revealed nothing particularly new. *The Lost Fairy Tale*, based on the relation between stage and film from the first programs of Laterna Magika, successfully entertained children for a number of years both at home and, later, in Canada.

I knew that if we were to progress any further, we would have to create a real theatre out of Laterna Magika. Moreover, it would need to be a repertory theatre, in which we would attempt to expand and deepen its current expressive resources and potential in order to validate the principles on which Laterna Magika was founded. It was clear to me that any progress would depend, first of all, on its dramaturgy.

116

In 1976, with director Evald Schorm and, later, directors Jan Švankmajer and Jiří Srnec, we began to prepare the program for *The Magical Circus*, on a theme suggested by Schorm. It was the first time that we attempted a more coherent narrative and also the first time that basic, familiar feelings and states of mind—love, joy, sadness, longing, envy, playfulness, maliciousness, naïvete, shrewdness—were presented by a childishly simple

are especially effective. As of April 17, 1987, the tenth anniversary of its premiere, *The Magical Circus* had over 2,500 performances at home and abroad. It's easy to imagine how difficult it is to maintain the quality of a performance repeated so often. We managed to do it thanks to periodic turnovers in casting (almost the entire cast of dancers was changed since the premiere), to the fact that the individual roles allow for an almost infinite

Offenbach. Tales of Hoffmann. *Laterna Magika, Prague, 1962. Dir: Václav Kašlík.*

but stylistically complex form of repetition.

We chose scenes from the life of two clowns, proceeding from their fable-like birth to their jolly as well as distressful search for an eternally transformable and eternally unattainable Venus. Finally they came to terms with the fact that the ideal remained an ideal while life had fled.

The scenography emphasized the naïvete of the material; it was created by a few properties and a panorama, as well as a projection surface of circus canvas, raised and lowered in various ways by stagehands in full view of the audience. The music, mostly derivative, often a persiflage, and full of easily recallable motifs for each of the main characters, also strengthened the unity of style, as did the costumes of Zdenek Seydl. The technical "miracle" lay merely in shooting the picture with three cameramen at once, in six-channel sound reproduction, and, with regard to interpretation, in the precise interplay of film and stage action.

We confirmed once again that a realistic cinematic image is inappropriate for Laterna Magika: on the contrary, larger than life details and the greatest stylization

number of variations within basic patterns and within the creative contribution of the performers, and finally to a sustained insistence on the quality of each performance. It's also true that we shortened *The Magical Circus* twice during those ten years, achieving a more effective rhythmic balance.

We often wondered about the reasons for its extraordinary reception at home and abroad. A six-week guest appearance in Barrault's theatre in Paris in 1984 was a distinct success with both the public and the critics, as had also been true in Holland, Belgium, the USSR, the USA, the German Federal Republic, Italy, and Bulgaria. We decided, simply, that it orchestrates familiar and understandable feelings in an unusually effective whole.

In 1979, director Schorm and I attempted an out and out epic story—Andersen's *Snow Queen*. I broke up what had been a total image on the circus canvas of *The Magical Circus* into a series of images that emerged from the darkness and disappeared into it once again. We worked with enlarged details and kinetic scenery that fluidly changed the stage space.

The filmed portion was evocative, but the problem was

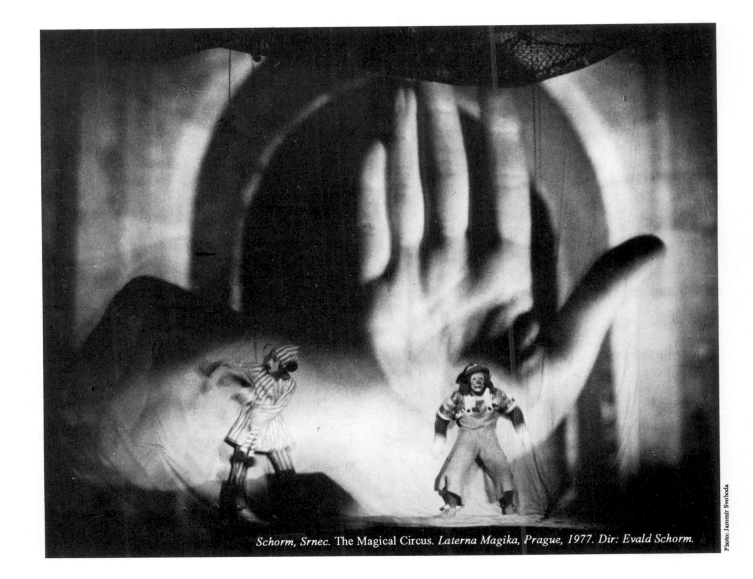

Schorm, Srnec. The Magical Circus. *Laterna Magika, Prague, 1977. Dir: Evald Schorm.*

Folta. The Lost Fairy Tale. *Laterna Magika, Prague, 1975. Dir: Jaromil Jireš.*

clearly the relation between film and stage. In some passages they reinforced one another, but there were more than a few sequences during which the filmed image and the stage action simply stood next to each other without dramatic contact. We played it for five years and it won grateful audiences, young and old, but it didn't reveal how to progress after *The Magical Circus*.

In 1981, we tried using television in Laterna Magika's first production of straight drama. Antonin Máša wrote an original play for us, the place of action being our very own theatre; television became one of the characters. We had four cameras: one shot the backstage area and three the stage. The director of the production cut from one to another to send appropriate shots to a large monitor placed on stage. We used these shots to juxtapose action backstage with action on stage. They also allowed the viewer to observe important reactions on the monitor, such as an actor who had his back turned to the audience, or the behavior of onstage characters who were not directly involved in the immediate action. Anyone on stage could be seen on the monitor at any given moment in a blown-up closeup. This created a special tension by the suggestion that a *Night Rehearsal*, as the play was called, was really going on, and that it was being shot precisely at that moment by television. Viewers felt present at a unique event. The scenography itself was adapted to this fictive reality; strictly functional, it seemed almost absent from the stage. The play (directed by Evald Schorm) was extraordinarily successful with audiences. We withdrew it

from the repertoire only after the tragic death of one of the chief performers, Ivan Lut'anský.

We used television technology a second time in 1987— this time joined with film—in Máša's second play, *Vivisection.* All the action was set in a television studio. The film presented documentary shots directly involved with the action itself and important experiences from the hero's life. The television camera took shots only of the hero, unbeknownst to him. The television reporting forced on the viewer the truth about the hero and his life. The author himself took over the direction of his play.

An entirely different encounter between dramatic text and the polyphonic vision of Laterna Magika occurred in the dramatization of Chekhov's short story *The Black Monk* (dramatization Jiří Fried, direction Evald Schorm). Here, kinetic scenography and the filmed images projected onto it created an honest atmosphere of the environment in which the action took place. The actors and the filmed images were never juxtaposed. The aim of the creators was to have their efforts convey a genuine impression of changes of place, time, and inner, spiritual movement.[1]

In Laterna Magika's first attempt at an opera, *The Tales of Hoffmann* (1962), Václav Kašlík and I used singers on stage as well as actors with voiceovers on the screen. In our second operatic venture, *The Talkative Snail* by Jiří Pauer (direction Břetislav Pojar, camera Jan Kališ), we used voiceovers consistently and the action took place entirely on the stage, while filmed images on my scenography created a fairy-tale environment. It became evident that this approach was not a dead end, and that certain types of opera would actually welcome it.

My greatest risk with Laterna Magika was our adaptation of Homer's *Odyssey.* Our presentation of *Odysseus* was prepared for the Palace of Culture in Prague and other large assembly halls all over the world. Because it was impossible to rehearse in our small theatre, we had to adapt a former movie theatre on our own, with difficulties that still give us bad dreams.

Once again we started from one of the most basic Laterna Magika principles: the necessity of creating familiar emotional situations with several levels of meaning, filling them with contemporary, equally familiar signs derived from stage, music, and film. We took the story of Odysseus the man, whose understanding of meaningful human values is restricted by his world as well as his own limitations. Since all fundamental questions on the meaning of human behavior had been already provided by Homer, we tried only to interpret them in the most understandable manner. The authors of the scenario were Evald Schorm, Jaroslav Kučera, Jindřich Smetana, Michael Kocáb; the director was Evald Schorm. Jindřich Smetana was the designer for the filmed portion, Michael Kocáb the composer, Ondrej Šoth the choreographer, and Šárka Hejnová (my daughter) the costume designer.

My scenography consisted of vertical scaffolding covered by a surface that curved out to blend with the stage floor, with openings for the entrances of actors at several levels. The scaffolding was accessible from the rear and its surface was used for both frontal projections and live action. The scaffolding also afforded storage space for all the properties. Beyond this, there was only a mobile platform, containing a small, unfolding gangplank, that was suspended from cables and driven by electrical motors in the flies. It was the boat of Odysseus and his company, and also another projection surface. We thought that large-screen, maximally stylized images tightly bound to the onstage action would, in an age of videocassettes, be the most effective means toward our ends. Furthermore, Homer's prototypical story allowed us to move within the timeless, universally familiar emotive history of European humanity.

Laterna Magika is over thirty years old, which may not seem like much, but for a theatre that has remained the sole example of its type during all those years, it is an epoch. We have experimented and discovered a good deal in that time, especially during the last decade, but we also know we're still at the very beginning.

Those who work at Laterna Magika in the future must realize that, each and every time, they begin an unbelievably demanding adventure from ground zero, not knowing its outcome until the very last moment. They enter upon the adventure of discovering the secret network of relations between humanity and the world around it.[2]

EPILOGUE

The basic text of *The Secret of Theatrical Space* was completed by 1988. However, in view of the dramatic events that have transformed his country since the Velvet Revolution of November 1989, some personal statement that would suggest Svoboda's perspective, his sense of himself and his work since the original composition of this book seemed in order. The following is that statement, dated July 28, 1992.

—*J.M.B.*

I deliberated a long time whether to go along with the suggestion that I provide an updated reckoning of my work and say something about its overall direction. As a professor I am aware that even though it is impossible to transmit one's experience in any direct way in art, and finally even in life, it may be possible indirectly—by means of those experiences—to encourage those who are perceptive to follow their own, original paths, each as unrepeatable as mine has been.

I was born in the first years of the Czechoslovak Republic. I encountered theatre during the Second World War, when stage and audience mutually understood spoken and gestural signs of resistance. Even then I had already found my own hardheaded path, which I never abandoned.

Like most of my generation I believed that after the war it would be possible to build a better world, in which liberated art would reign. Like most of my generation I experienced disillusionment and disappointment, and like most I accepted November 1989 as a relief and a new promise.

Needless to say, my life as a citizen influenced my artistic development to the extent that it stimulated me to find my own form of expression, my own coming to terms with reality. No one, least of all an artist, can live outside the era in which it has been his lot to live. Even though he may wish ever so intensely to be detached, and even though at first glance he may succeed, it is still only a form of reacting to that era. I always attempted a dialogue with it, successfully or unsuccessfully. I'm an architect and a scenographer, and an intense receptivity to my time has always been the seedbed of my work. Now, just as at the beginning of my work, I believe that the world and humanity stand at a crossroads before salvation or annihilation.

If my story prompts the thought that neither slogans nor ideological programs provide salvation, but that one of the *roads* to salvation may be a humble search for the point in which the spirit of the art of the past meets the as yet unknown spirit of the present, I'll be glad.

Svoboda in the mid-1970s in historic Teatro Olympico, Vicenza, Italy.

121

FOOTNOTES

Scenography

[1] As in other sections of the book, here Svoboda describes what seems to be a distinct foreshadowing of postmodern deconstruction, although he and his colleagues never rejected fairly traditional notions of aesthetic unity and coherence. (Unless otherwise indicated, all footnotes are mine. JMB)

[2] The Cologne *Tristan* was a further refinement of the technique employed earlier (1967) in the Wiesbaden *Tristan*.

[3] Since Svoboda wrote these words (1988), Laterna Magika has entered a new phase of its history. In 1992, negotiations were completed to detach Laterna Magika from the National Theatre and make it an autonomous, virtually self-supporting unit under the Ministry of Culture.

Until 1945

[1] The reference is to a special lighting instrument (usually ganged in clusters of five or nine) that employs low voltage to cast an unusually intense beam of focused backlighting from a high, upstage position down toward the apron. The effect is to create a halo-like effect on actors or objects it strikes, as well as to create a wall or curtain of light, especially if the light passes through air that is heavy with dust or vapor.

[2] In late September and early October of 1938, decisive meetings were held in Munich between Hitler and representatives of Britain (Neville Chamberlain) and France (Eduard Daladier) regarding the fate of the Sudetenland territories of Czechoslovakia, which were being claimed by Hitler for his Third Reich. The British and French rather ignobly capitulated to Hitler's demands, without bothering to consult with Czechoslovakia. The Second Republic refers to the new government in Czechoslovakia following the Munich capitulation; it lasted from October 1938 to March 15, 1939, when Hitler's armies invaded and occupied (without opposition) what remained of the Czech and Moravian lands. On the 17th of November, 1939, as a gesture of intimidation, German forces executed nine university students, and all universities were closed until the end of the war. (Although it occurred after Svoboda completed the text of this book, it is worth noting that on November 17, 1989, a peaceful march of students to commemorate the fiftieth anniversary of this event was assaulted by riot police very close to the National Theatre. This latter encounter triggered the Velvet Revolution that led to the overthrow of the Communist regime.)

[3] For three days, May 5-8, 1945, at the end of World War II, the citizens of Prague openly rebelled against the German forces of occupation, setting up barricades and otherwise harassing the Germans as the Soviet and American armies were approaching the capital. Svoboda briefly led an improvised, armed brigade during the uprising.

The Theatre of the Fifth of May

[1] Václav Kašlík died in 1990.

[2] Svoboda designed an entirely new production of *Rusalka* that opened in January 1991.

[3] Šárka Hejnová is now a well-regarded freelance costume designer who occasionally collaborates with Svoboda.

[4] An ironic completion of a circle occurred on April 1, 1992, when the Smetana Theatre once again became an autonomous producing ensemble directly under the Ministry of Culture. It is now known as the State Opera.

The National Theatre

[1] The reference is to thin, very pliable plastic sheets in varying monochromatic shades (mostly from white to black) which function as projection surfaces for slide or cinematic film; some folios are designed for frontal projection, some for rear projection, and some for both; they also vary according to their angles of dispersion or reflection.

[2] For Svoboda, one of the most painful effects of the political pressures following the crushing of the Prague Spring of 1968 was his loss of control of the National Theatre workshops in the early 1970s. He remained as chief designer but was no longer head of technical operations.

[3] Vychodil's set was a small bullring or bearpit of rough boards and a dirt floor, with upper benches for the revolutionary mob that reviled the French aristocrats within.

Opera

[1] Subsequent to the Velvet Revolution of 1989, this eighteenth-century theatre was re-designated the Estates Theatre, which had been its name in the nineteenth and early twentieth centuries.

[2] In the summer of 1988 in the ancient Roman theatre at Orange in the south of France, Svoboda and director J. C. Riber mounted yet another complete *Ring* cycle.

Artistic Collaboration Abroad

[1] Tovstonogov died in 1989.

[2] It would be more accurate to say that the Novosibirsk *Jenufa* was Svoboda's first foreign production with a foreign director. *Jenufa* was preceded by two other productions abroad, but with a Czech director. In April 1956 he teamed with Václav Kašlík on a production of the latter's *Janošík* at the State Opera of Dresden, GDR; and in January 1958, again with Kašlík, on Dvorak's *Rusálka* at the La Fenice theatre in Venice.

[3] John Dexter died in 1990.

[4] Two years later, in 1970, Svoboda worked with Olivier on a film version of *The Three Sisters*, which subsequently received a prize from the Los Angeles critics for its scenography.

[5] The Strehler-Svoboda *Faust* I was presented in 1988; *Faust* II was presented in 1991.

The Exhibition as World Outlook

[1] It was less than one year after the occupation of Czechoslovakia by the Soviet led Warsaw Pact armies; this exhibit was clearly meant to reinforce a sense of national culture and identity.

Laterna Magika

[1] The entire presentation of *The Black Monk* was bought by the Hillberry Theatre in Detroit and presented by American actors in October 1986. Neither *The Black Monk* nor *Vivisection* was designed by Svoboda.

[2] Laterna Magika's most recent production (1990) was *Minotaurus*, based on a poetic text by Friedrich Dürrenmatt and directed (but not designed) by Svoboda himself. Its next production, scheduled to open by early 1993, is based on Mozart's *The Magic Flute*.

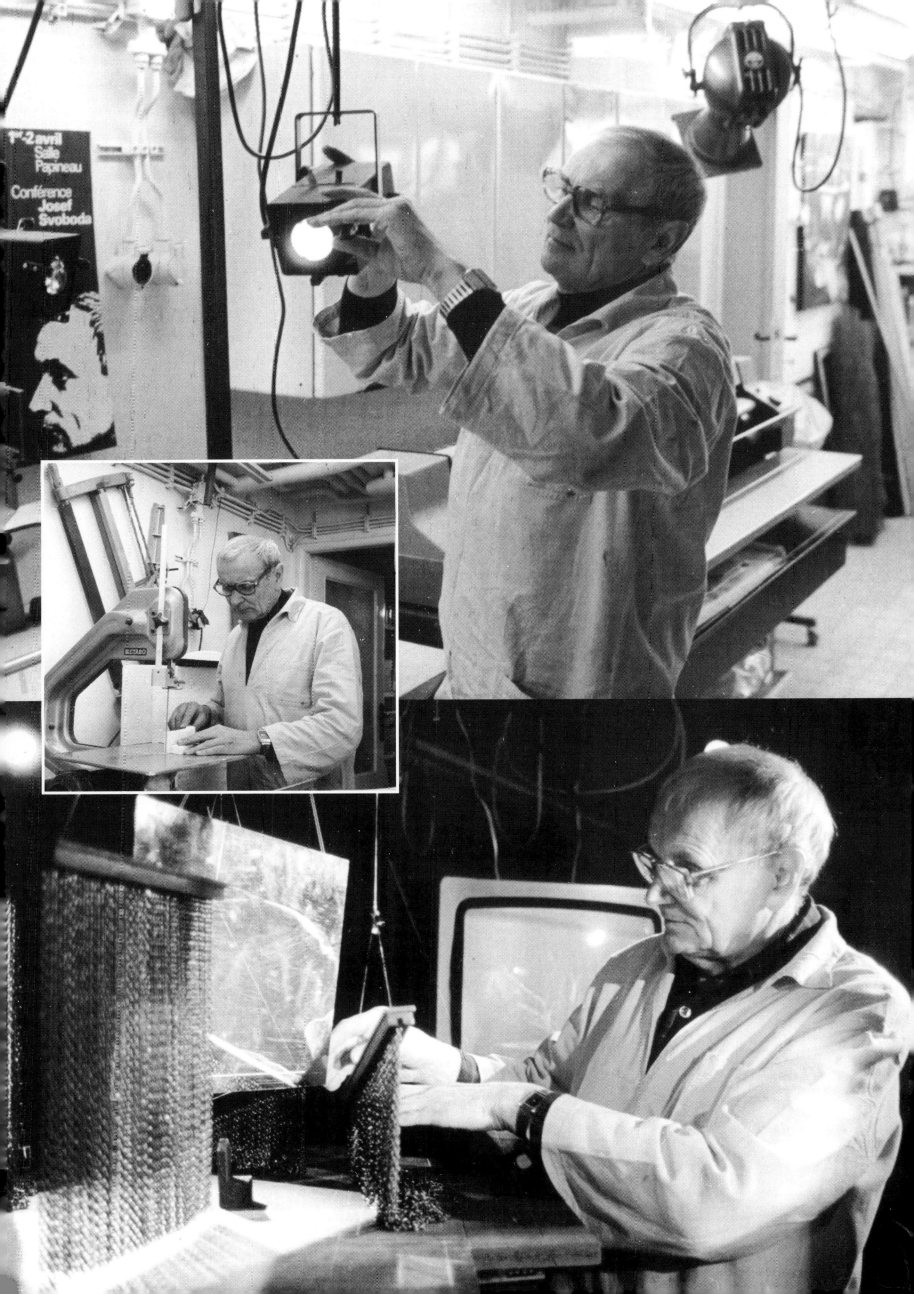

GLOSSARY
OF KEY NAMES AND TERMS

Aleš, Mikuláš (1852-1912). A Czech painter of the Romantic era whose works drew heavily from Czech history, legend, and folk sources.

Brussels Expo 58. The reference is to the international exposition of 1958, Brussels Expo 58, at which the Czech pavilion drew very favorable attention. It was here that two of Svoboda's major innovations, Polyekran and Laterna Magika, had their first public exposure.

Burian, E.F. (1904-1959). Educated as a composer, Burian entered theatre as an actor and musician. He became the leading Czech leftist, avant-garde director of the 1930s, especially noted for developing his own scenarios, making extensive use of music as a principle of staging, and integrating filmed projections into his *mise en scènes*.

Čapek brothers. Karel (1890-1938), a major novelist and Czechoslovakia's most important playwright prior to World War II; his work has been referred to as philosophic and poetic science fiction. *R.U.R.*, *The Insect Comedy*, and *The Makropulos Affair* are probably his best known plays. **Josef** (1887-1945), collaborated on several plays with Karel, but was more important as painter and stage designer during the 1920s and 1930s.

Dramaturg. Usually a regular staff position in virtually every European repertory theatre. The dramaturg is a literary specialist who acts as advisor and consultant on all plays (or operas) being done by a theatre. The dramaturg is responsible for providing the director and actors with all relevant information on the background of the work under consideration, including critical and theoretical studies relating to the work and its author. Such information also provides the basis of publicity and program copy. The dramaturg may become a very significant figure in a theatre, playing a key role in the development of a long-range repertory philosophy

Erben, Karel Jaromír (1811-1870). A major folklorist and poet whose work reflects the Romantic era's interest in legend, myth, and folk material.

Forman, Miloš (1932-) The celebrated Czech filmmaker, who gained international attention when his *Loves of a Blond* won an Oscar in 1965, was one of a number of young film artists who collaborated on the early programs of Laterna Magika.

Frejka, Jiří (1904-1952). A major Czech director whose career spanned the 1920s to the early 1950s; he began with avant-garde work in small Prague theatres but eventually became a leading director in the National Theatre and, after World War II, in the Vinohrady Theatre.

Gottlieb, Václav (1904-1951). A scene and costume designer who was head of production logistics at the National Theatre from 1943 until his death in 1951.

Götz, František (1894-1974). A significant force in the National Theatre as a dramaturg and as head of drama at different periods from the 1930s to the late 1960s; he was also a professor of drama at Charles University after World War II.

Hilar, Karel Hugo (1885-1935). The leading Czech stage director from 1917 until his death. He worked as head of drama at both of Prague's large repertory theatres, the Vinohrady and the National. His bold, often expressionistic staging brought Czech theatre into the mainstream of contemporary European theatre.

Hofman, Vlastislav (1884-1964). The dominant Czech stage designer of the first third of the twentieth century. Trained as an architect, he was at his best in large-scale productions at both the Vinohrady and National theatres, where he was Hilar's chief collaborator.

Honzl, Jindřich (1894-1953). An important avant-garde director of surrealistic plays in the years between the wars, he became head of drama at the National Theatre after World War II. Honzl was also a notable critic and theorist of drama and film.

Hrdlička, Bohumil (1919-1990). An innovative young director with whom Svoboda worked on numerous productions in Ostrava and later at the National Theatre in Prague, in the first decade after the war.

Hrubín, František (1910-1971). A poet who also wrote several interesting plays in his later years, such as *A Sunday in August* and *Oldřich and Božena*.

Janáček, Leoš (1854-1928). The greatest Czech composer of the twentieth century; his operas have increasingly become staples of the international opera repertoire.

Jirásek, Alois (1851-1930). A major historical novelist but less notable dramatist in the epic vein, dedicated to the nationalist aspirations of the Czechs.

Kačer, Jan (1936-). An important director (also an actor) since the mid-1960s both in smaller, studio theatres as well as larger repertory theatres, including the National Theatre.

Karnet, Jiří (1920-). An author who was one of Svoboda's early collaborators. He emigrated to the United States in 1948.

Kašlík, Václav (1917-1989). He was a driving force in the establishment of the Theatre of the Fifth of May and subsequently developed into a successful international opera director and conductor, as well as Svoboda's most frequent directorial collaborator.

Kohout, Eduard (1889-1976). A leading actor of the National Theatre for decades, he was especially effective in lyrical, sophisticated roles.

Kouřil, Miroslav (1911-1984). A stage designer with a strong interest in technical and lighting aspects of staging. He was E.F. Burian's chief collaborator, and later headed the Scenografic Laboratory; his last years were spent as Professor of Theatre Studies at Charles University.

Krejča, Otomar (1921-). At first an actor, he worked under both E.F. Burian and Jiří Frejka after World War II. Subsequently he was regarded, along with Alfred Radok, as the chief postwar Czech director, most notable for his work at the National Theatre and, later, his own Theatre Beyond the Gate. Svoboda designed virtually all of Krejča's major work through 1972, when Krejča was forced to close his Gate theatre. Currently, after years of exile, Krejča is once again directing in Prague.

Lukavský, Radovan (1919-). A major Czech actor during the postwar era, at the National Theatre since 1957; he specializes in roles demanding thoughtfulness, decisiveness, and ethical complexity.

Mácha, Karel Hynek (1810-1836). The Czech Byron, he lived a short, intense life that encapsulated the major themes of Romanticism in its more hectic aspects; his major work is a lyrical poem of epic scale, *Máj (May)*.

Macháček, Miroslav (1922-1991). An intense, dynamic actor and director, he joined the National Theatre in 1959 and collaborated with Svoboda on many highly admired productions.

Martinů, Bohuslav (1890-1959). The leading Czech composer of the generation following Leoš Janáček. Strongly influenced by modern French music and literature, he nevertheless sustained his native roots even though living abroad after 1923. His works for theatre include numerous ballets and operas.

Medřická, Dana (1920-1983). A character actress of great expressiveness, she was a member of the National Theatre from 1959. Blanche Dubois and Mother Courage were among her notable roles.

Mrštík brothers, Alois (1861-1925) and **Vilem** (1863-1912). Novelists in the nineteenth-century realistic tradition, they collaborated on the powerful naturalistic tragedy of village life, *Maryša*, in 1894.

Němcová, Božena (1820-1862). The first important Czech woman author, in whose works Romantic folk motifs and love of nature are prominent.

New Scene, The. The latest addition (1987) to the theatres composing the National Theatre complex, it was designed to accomodate relatively small-scale dramas, thus leaving opera, ballet, and large drama productions to the larger National Theatre buildings: the Smetana, the Tyl, and *the* National Theatre on the banks of the Vltava (Moldau). The Laterna Magika often made use of it, and as of the fall of 1992, it will be Laterna Magika's home base.

Pešek, Ladislav (1906-1986). A highly talented and popular character actor at the National Theatre from 1928 until the late 1970s; his forte was comedic character roles in which he could make full use of his gifts for mime and almost acrobatic physicalization. Among his major achievements were the roles of the Tramp in *The Insect Comedy*, Polonius in *Hamlet*, and

Archie Rice in *The Entertainer*.

Pleskot, Jaromír (1922-). A director who worked under both E.F. Burian and Jiří Frejka, Pleskot joined the National Theatre in 1957. He was particularly successful in bringing a fresh, non-academic approach to classics as well as to contemporary plays, on many of which he collaborated with Svoboda.

Radok, Alfred (1914-1976). According to many, perhaps the most gifted and creatively individualistic of the postwar Czech directors. He was an assistant under E.F. Burian in the early years of the occupation, one of the founders of the Theatre of the Fifth of May, and a director at the National Theatre during several periods starting in 1954. He went into voluntary exile immediately after the August 1968 Warsaw Pact invasion, worked mainly as guest director in Sweden, and died in Vienna while guest directing there in 1976.

Salzer, František (1902-1974). A director at both the Theatre of the Fifth of May and at the National Theatre (1947-1963), Salzer was also an influential teacher of directing from 1945-1974 at the Academy of Dramatic Art in Prague.

Šamberk, František (1838-1904). A member of the National Theatre from the early 1880s, Šamberk was primarily a very popular actor and occasional director, who also wrote a number of lively farces.

School of Applied and Industrial Arts (Vysoká Škola Umělecko-Průmyslová or UMPRUM). This is a university-level school that trains architects, graphic artists, and craftsmen in ceramics, glass, and other media. Svoboda received his formal training in architecture here; subsequently, he joined the faculty as a professor of architecture in 1969 and retired in 1990.

Schorm, Evald (1931-1988). Originally trained in the Film Academy, Schorm later became primarily active as a stage director in the 1970s and 1980s in numerous studio and regional theatres, and also frequently collaborated with Svoboda as director and scenarist for Laterna Magika productions.

Smetana, Bedřich (1824-1884) He is the Czech composer most closely identified with the traditions and spirit of his native land. Not only drawing on Czech history and legend for his major operas, he also was intensely active in nationalistic efforts toward greater autonomy in the nineteenth century. This activity centered in his years-long efforts to establish a National Theatre. Fittingly enough, the initial work performed at the opening of the National Theatre in 1883 was his opera *Libuše*, based on a heroic Czech legend. This opera is still traditionally performed at the opening of each National Theatre season.

Theatre of the Fifth of May. A theatre launched in 1945 immediately after the second World War by a group of young literary, musical, and theatre artists, with most of whom Svoboda had been associated during the war years. The group had the great good fortune of being given the former German theatre in Prague.

Thein, Hanuš (1904-1974). An opera singer and director, Thein was a member of the National Theatre from 1929 until his death, functioning as Head of Opera on several occasions. He often collaborated with Svoboda in the 1950s and 1960s.

Topol, Josef (1935-). Regarded by many as the most gifted of Czech playwrights after World War II, he became the resident playwright of the creative team headed by Krejča in the National Theatre and the Theatre Beyond the Gate. His works were banned from the early 1970s to 1989.

Trnka, Jiří (1912-1969). A painter and incidental stage and costume designer, Trnka is best known for his creative work in animated Czech films of fairy tales and legends.

Tröster, František (1904-1968). A highly influential stage designer and teacher from the 1930s to the 1960s, he bridged the eras between Vlastislav Hofman and Svoboda. Like them, he was also trained as an architect.

Tyl, Josef Kajetan (1808-1856). An unusually gifted, versatile man of literature and theatre, a critic, editor, and parliamentary representative, as well as playwright, actor, and director, Tyl was a significant figure in inspiring the nationalist movement of the mid-nineteenth century and in making theatre a significant force in Czech life. His contributions were recognized in the renaming of Prague's oldest theatre, the former Estates Theatre, in his honor after World War II. The theatre, however, was renamed (again) the Estates Theatre after the 1989 Velvet Revolution.

Vychodil, Ladislav (1920-). Svoboda's contemporary and peer, Vychodil, a student of Tröster, has been the leading scenographer in Slovak theatre since World War II. He has also worked extensively in Czech theatre and abroad, and he established the scenographic division in the Bratislava Academy of Theatre Art in 1951. He did several striking, highly imaginative productions with Alfred Radok in the 1960s.

THE COMPLETE REGISTER OF SVOBODA
PRODUCTIONS
1943-1992

THEATRE KEY

ABCT	ABC Theatre	MAT	Moscow Art Theatre	SfT	Semafor Theatre
AT	Academic Theatre	MCT	Municipal Chamber Theatre	SM	Smetana Museum
BeT	Berlin Tournament	ML	Municipal Library	SMT	Smetana Theatre
BT	Burgtheater	MM	Municipal Museum	SNT	Slovak National Theatre
CG	Covent Garden	MO	Metropolitan Opera	SO	State Opera
ChT	Chamber Theatre	MT	Municipal Theatre	SOT	Stanislavsky Opera Theatre
CNT	Croatian National Theatre	NAC	National Arts Center	ST	State Theatre
COH	Civic Opera House	NC	Nuremberg Castle	SUNY	State University of N.Y.
CP	Congress Palace	NO	National Opera	T5M	Theatre of the Fifth of May
CR	Conservatoire Royal	NS	Nemzeti Szinhas	TA	Theatre Academy
D49	Theatre 49	NST	New Satire Theatre	TaG	Theatre am Gartnerplatz
DSK	Disk Theatre	NT	National Theatre	TB	Theatre on the Ballustrade
DT	Deutches Theatre	NTs	National Theatre Studio	TBG	Theatre Beyond the Gate
EFBT	E.F. Burian Theatre	NwT	New Theatre	TC	Teatro Communale
ET	Eisenhower Theatre	Od	Odeon	TCA	Theatre of the Czech Army
EX58	EXPO 58	OGB	Opera Group of Boston	TG	Tourneetheatre greve
EX67	EXPO 67	OH	Opera House	TGV	Teatro Giuseppe Verdi
FT	Festival Theatre	OST	Oldrich Stibor Theatre	TL	Theatre Liberte
GO	Grand Opera	OT	Opera Theatre	TLF	Teatro La Fenice
GpT	Goetheplatz Theatre	PC	Palais congress	TM	Teatro Mella
GT	Grand Opera	PR	Plexus S.R.L. Roma	TPC	Theatre Espace Pierre Cardin
HNT	Het National Ballet	PS	Piccolo Scala	TRF	Teatro Romano Fiesole
HO	Houston Opera	QET	Queen Elizabeth Theatre	TRg	Teatro Reggio
HT	Horacke Theatre	RaT	Raamtheatre	TRo	Theatre Royal
JK	Jara Kohout Theatre	RkT	Rokoko Theatre	TS	Theatre Studio
JS	Julliard School	RmT	Roman Theatre	TStb	Teatro Stabile
KC	Kennedy Center	ROH	Royal Opera House	TSB	Teatro San Babila
KIT	Karlin Theatre	RT	Regional Theatre	TT	Tyl Theatre
KO	Komische Opera	SAT	Satire Theatre	TW	Teatr Wielki
KT	King's Theatre	SC	State Conservatory	TYP	Theatre of Young Pioneers
LC	Lincoln Center	ScT	Schiller Theatre	VB	Volksbuhn
LM	Laterna Magika	SINT	Slovene National Theatre	VO	Volksopera
LS	La Scala	SFT	State Film Theatre	ZNT	Zdenek Nejedly Theatre

AUTHOR	TITLE	CITY	THEATRE	DATE	DIRECTOR
Hölderlin, F.	*Empedocles*	Prague	SM	1943	Karnet, J.
Strindberg, A.	*Crown Bride*	Prague	SM	1943	Weis, I.
Behounek, K.	*John, the Page*	Prague	JK	1943	Sonnevend, C.
Billinger, R.	*Fox Trap*	Prague	MT	1943	Kandert, J.
Weis, I.	*Peddlers' Songs*	Prague	ML	1944	Weis, I.
Tyl, J. K.	*Marianka, Mother of the Regiment* (n.p.)	Prague	SC	1944	Weis, I.
Karnet J.	*Astray* (not performed)	Prague	MT	1944	Salzer, F.
Ostrčil, O.	*Kunala's Eyes*	Prague	T5M	1945	Fiedler, J.
Nezval, V.	*Manon Lescaut*	Teplice	MT	1946	Šeřinský, T.
Martens, G., Obey, A.	*Wastrels in Paradise*	Prague	NTS	1946	Vyskočil, S.
Jirásek, A.	*Jan Roháč*	Teplice	MT	1946	Šeřinský, T.
Offenbach, J.	*Tales of Hoffmann*	Prague	T5M	1946	Radok, A.
Dyk, V.	*Andre and the Dragon*	Jihlava	HT	1946	Vyskočil, S.
Mascagni, F.	*Cavaleria Rusticana*	Ostrava	ST	1946	Hrdlička, B.
Leoncavallo, R.	*Pagliacci*	Ostrava	ST	1946	Hrdlička, B.
Smetana, B.	*Bartered Bride*	Prague	T5M	1946	Kašlik, V.
Kainar, J.	*Aibiš's Action*	Prague	SAT	1946	Radok, A.
Čapek, K. and J.	*Insect Comedy*	Prague	NT	1946	Honzl, J.
Shaw, G. B.	*Women's Sufferage*	Prague	DSK	1946	Weis, I.

Author	Title	City	Theatre	Date	Director
Janáček, L.	*Káta Kabanová*	Prague	T5M	1947	Kašlík, V.
Gounod, C.	*Faust*	Pilsen	TT	1947	Mráz, L.
Verdi, G.	*Aida*	Prague	T5M	1947	Kašlík, V.
Maeterlinck, M.	*Mayor of Stilmond*	Prague	T5M	1947	Radok, A.
Žák, J.	*Purge*	Prague	SAT	1947	Radok, A.
Radok, A.	*Strange Adventures*	Prague	TYP	1947	Radok, A.
Puccini, G.	*Tosca*	Prague	T5M	1947	Jernek, K.
Hába, A.	*Mother*	Prague	T5M	1947	Fiedler, J.
Verdi, G.	*Trovatore*	Prague	T5M	1947	Fiedler, J.
Blázek, V.	*King Dislikes Beef*	Prague	SAT	1947	Lipský, O.
Tyl, J. K.	*Devil on Earth*	Prague	T5M	1947	Vyskočil, S.
Prokofiev, S.	*Engagement in the Cloister*	Prague	T5M	1947	Kašlík, V.
Offenbach, J.	*Tales of Hoffmann*	Ostrava	ST	1947	Hrdlička, B.
Verdi, G.	*Rigoletto*	Prague	T5M	1947	Radok A.
Massenet, J.	*Don Quixote*	Bratislava	SNT	1947	Fiedler, J.
Chopin, F.	*Ballet* (not performed)	Prague	T5M	1947	Kašlík, V.
Hellman, L.	*Little Foxes*	Prague	NT	1948	Radok, A.
Janáček, L.	*Travels of Mr. Brouček*	Prague	T5M	1948	Fiedler, J.
Gogol, N.	*Revizor*	Prague	NT	1948	Honzl, J.
Verdi, G.	*Otello*	Ostrava	ST	1948	Hrdlička, B.
de Falla, M.	*El Amor Brujo*	Prague	T5M	1948	Kašlík, V.
Leoncavallo, R.	*Pagliacci*	Prague	T5M	1948	Radok, A.
Horníček, M.	*Circus of Hopes*	Prague	SAT	1948	Horníček, M.
Novák, V.	*Nikotina*	Prague	T5M	1948	Jirsíková, N.
Puccini, G.	*Boheme*	Bratislava	SNT	1948	Fiedler, J.
Kašlík, V.	*Rogue's Ballad*	Prague	T5M	1948	Kašlík, V.
Blodek, V.	*In the Well*	Prague	T5M	1948	Fiedler, J.
Tobiáš, J.	*Golden Wedding*	Prague	NwT	1948	Hanuš, F.
Smetana, B.	*Devil's Wall*	Ostrava	ST	1948	Hrdlička, B.
Lahola, L.	*Ours Went This Way*	Prague	D49	1948	Weis, I.
Mrštík, A. and V.	*Maryša*	Prague	NT	1948	Honzl J.

Svoboda with director Alfred Radok

AUTHOR	TITLE	CITY	THEATRE	DATE	DIRECTOR
Karel, P.	*Grandad's Three Hairs*	Prague	NT	1948	Fiedler, J.
Leonov, L.	*Apple Orchard*	Prague	TT	1948	Nedbal, M.
Vomáčka, B.	*Water Sprite*	Prague	SMT	1948	Kašlík, V.
Puccini G.	*Boheme*	Ústí	ZNT	1948	Jedlička, R.
Fredro, A.	*Revenge* (not performed)			1948	Radok, A.
Krička, J.	*Czech Manger*	Prague	SMT	1949	Kašlík, V.
Klíma, J.	*Flaming Border*	Prague	TT	1949	Radok, A.
Pogodin, N.	*Aristocrats*	Prague	SFT	1949	Stejskal, B.
Balic, A., Isajv, K.	*Tajmir Calling*	Prague	D49	1949	Weis, I.
Jirásek, A.	*Lantern*	Prague	NT	1949	Pehr, J.
Martinů B.	*Spalíček*	Prague	SMT	1949	Jirsíková, N.
Khatchaturian, A.	*Carnival*	Prague	SMT	1949	Braun, R.
Ostrčil, O.	*Vlasta's Death*	Brno	ST	1949	Fiedler, J.
Stech, V.	*Wedding Under the Umbrellas*	Prague	NST	1949	Horníček, M.
Kapr, J.	*Revolutionary Suite*	Prague	SMT	1949	Braun, R.
Mozart, W. A.	*Don Giovanni*	Ostrava	ST	1949	Hrdlička, B.
Faltiš, L. C.	*Bride of Chod*	Prague	TT	1949	Radok, A.

Author	Title	City	Theatre	Date	Director
Fibich, Z.	*Hedy*	Prague	SMT	1949	Thein, H.
Kovarovic, K.	*On the Old Bleaching Ground*	Prague	SMT	1949	Fiedler, J.
Mozart, W. A.	*Abduction from the Seraglio*	Prague	SMT	1949	Fiedler, J.
Sofronov, A.	*Moscow Character*	Prague	NT	1949	Honzl, J.
Mozart, W. A.	*Abduction from the Seraglio*	Bratislava	SNT	1950	Fiedler, J.
Tchaikovsky, P. I.	*Eugen Onegin*	Prague	NT	1950	Fiedler, J.
Mozart, W. A.	*Marriage of Figaro*	Ostrava	ST	1950	Hrdlička, B.
Mozart, W. A.	*Don Giovanni*	Prague	SMT	1950	Mandaus, L.
Dvořák, A.	*Rusalka*	Ostrava	ST	1950	Hrdlička, B.
Scerbasev	*Tobacco Captain*	Fidlovacka	NT	1950	Janáček, M.
Kvapil, J.	*May's Tale*	Prague	NT	1950	Kašlík, V.
Šamberk, F. F.	*Eleventh Commandment*	Prague	SFT	1950	Radok, A.
Bizet, G.	*Carmen*	Ostrava	ST	1950	Hrdlička, B.
Kašlík, V.	*Wonder of Love*	Liberec	RT	1950	Mrnák, G.
Verdi, G.	*Don Carlos*	Ostrava	ST	1950	Hrdlička, B.
Tchaikovsky, P. I.	*Slippers*	Prague	SMT	1950	Thein, H.
Fibich, Z.	*Šárka*	Ostrava	ST	1950	Hrdlička, B.
Mussorgsky, M. P.	*Boris Godunov*	Pilsen	TT	1951	Thein, H.
Tchaikovsky, P. I.	*Eugen Onegin*	Ostrava	ST	1951	Hylas, I.
Moniuszko, S.	*Halka*	Prague	SMT	1951	Merunowicz, J.
Beethoven, L.	*Fidelio*	Ostrava	ST	1951	Hrdlička, B.
Cun, T. D.	*South of the 38th*	Prague	TT	1951	Salzer, F.
Kovarovic, K.	*Psohlavci*	Prague	NT	1951	Kašlík, V.
German, J.	*It Happened One Autumn Night*	Prague	TCA	1951	Weis, I.
Smetana, B.	*Dalibor*	Jindřichuv	RT	1951	Thein, H.
Rimsky-Korsakov, N.	*Coq D'Or*	Ústí	ZNT	1951	Pilat, M.
Smetana, B.	*Dalibor*	Ostrava	ST	1951	Hrdlička, B.
Beethoven, L.	*Fidelio*	Bratislava	SNT	1951	Fiedler, J.
Tyl, J. K.	*Bagpiper of Strakonice*	Pilzen	TT	1951	Pistorius, L.
Mozart, W. A.	*Marriage of Figaro*	Opava	RT	1951	Kašlík, V.
Moliere	*Georges Dandin*	Prague	TT	1951	Nedbal, M.
Plautus	*Ghost Comedy* (not performed)	Prague	NT	1951	Salzer, F.
Mozart, W. A.	*Magic Flute* (not performed)	Ostrava	ST	1951	Hrdlička, B.
Weber, C. M. von	*Freischutz*	Prague	ST	1952	Kašlík, V.
Verdi, G.	*Masked Ball*	Ostrava	ST	1952	Hrdlička, B.
Jirásek, A.	*Lantern*	Prague	NT	1952	Boháč, L.
Verdi, G.	*Don Carlos*	Pilzen	TT	1952	Thein, H.
Shakespeare, W.	*Merry Wives of Windsor*	Pilzen	TT	1952	Hofbauer, Z.
Smetana, B.	*Brandenburgs in Bohemia*	Prague	NT	1952	Hrdlička, B.
Jariš, M.	*Pledge*	Prague	TCA	1952	Weis, I.
Tyl, J. K.	*Stubborn Woman*	Prague	TT	1952	Průcha, J.
Smetana, B.	*Secret*	Prague	NT	1952	Hrdlička, B.
Nestroy, J.	*Lumpáci Vagabundus*	Prague	KT	1952	Radok, A.
Dvořák, A.	*Devil and Kate*	Prague	ST	1952	Thein, H.
Prokofiev, S.	*Romeo and Juliet*	Pilzen	TT	1952	Němecěk, J.
Smetana, B.	*Bartered Bride*	Prague	NT	1953	Boháč, L.
Tyl, T. K.	*Miners of Kutná Hora*	Prague	TT	1953	Průcha, J.
Stroupežnický, L.	*Our Militants*	Prague	TT	1953	Štepánek, Z.
Suchoň, E.	*Whirlpool*	Prague	NT	1953	Hrdlička, B.
Stroupežnický, L.	*Our Militants*	Karlovy Vary	RT	1953	Stejskal, B.
Smetana, B.	*Bartered Bride*	Bratislava	SNT	1953	Kašlík, V.
Tchaikovsky, P. I.	*Eugen Onegin*	Prague.	ST	1953	Jedlička, R.
Tyl, J. K.	*Jan Hus*	Prague	TT	1953	Dvořák, A.
Smetana, B.	*Libuše*	Prague	NT	1953	Boháč, L.
Drda, J.	*Games with the Devil*	Prague	NT	1953	Salzer, F.
Mozart, W. A.	*Marriage of Figaro*	Prague	TT	1954	Hrdlička, B.
Mussorgsky, M. P.	*Boris Godunov*	Prague	NT	1954	Dombrovskij, N.
Gorky, M.	*Enemies*	Prague	NT	1954	Dudin, V.
Verdi, G.	*Rigoletto*	Prague	SMT	1954	Hrdlička, B.
Dvořák, A.	*Crafty Farmer*	Prague	SMT	1954	Radok, A.
Čapek, K.	*Robber*	Prague	TT	1954	Radok, A.
Shakespeare, W.	*Merchant of Venice*	Prague	NT	1954	Salzer, F.
Tetauer, F.	*Battle of Dragons*	Prague	MCT	1955	Vrbský, B.
Dvořák, A.	*Rusalka*	Prague	NT	1955	Hrdlička, B.

Author	Title	City	Theatre	Date	Director
Tolstoy, L.	*Fruits of Enlightenment*	Prague	TT	1955	Průcha, J.
Smetana, B.	*Bartered Bride*	Prague	NT	1955	Kašlík,V.
Jing, A	*Model King*	Prague	TT	1955	Štepánek, Z.
Stehlík. M.	*High Summer Sky*	Prague	TT	1955	Radok, A.
Tyl, J. K.	*Incendiary's Daughter*	Prague	TCA	1955	Strejček, J.
Chekhcv, A.	*Three Sisters*	Prague	TT	1955	Štepánek, Z.
Radok, A.	*It Happened in the Rain*	Prague	MT	1955	Radok, A.
Gounod, C.	*Faust*	Prague	NT	1955	Thein, H.
Zinner	*Devil's Circle*	Prague	TT	1955	Radok, A.
Mozart. W.A.	*Don Giovanni*	Prague	TT	1956	Mandaus, L.
Jirásek, A.	*Father*	Prague	NT	1956	Zelenský, D.
Verdi, G.	*Don Carlos*	Bratislava	SNT	1956	Wasserbauer, M.
Nezval,V.	*Today...Atlantida*	Prague	TT	1956	Radok, A.
Kašlík, V.	*Janošík*	Dresden	OH	1956	Kašlík, V.
Tyl, J. K.	*George's Vision*	Prague	TT	1956	Průcha, J.
Glinka, M. I.	*Ruslan and Ludmila*	Prague	NT	1956	Zacharov, R.
Mrštík, A. and V.	*Maryša*	Prague	NT	1956	Štepánek, Z.
Breal, P. A.	*Hussars*	Prague	SAT	1956	Horníček, M
Mozart. W. A.	*Magic Flute*	Prague	NT	1957	Hrdlička, B.
Tchaikovsky, P. I.	*Queen of Spades*	Prague	SMT	1957	Thein, H.
Leonov, L.	*Golden Carriage*	Prague	TT	1957	Radok, A.
Procházka, J.	*Dawn Above the Waters*	Prague	TCA	1957	Strejček, J.
Voskovec and Werich	*Helen's Happy*	Prague	ABCT	1957	Roháč, J.
deFillippo, E.	*Number One Fear*	Pilzen	TT	1957	Špídla, V.
Grieg, N.	*Defeat*	Prague	TT	1957	Pleskot, J.

Svoboda with director Václav Kašlík

AUTHOR	TITLE	CITY	THEATRE	DATE	DIRECTOR
Hellman. L.	*Autumn Garden*	Prague	TT	1957	Radok, A.
Galsworthy, J.	*Jungle*	Pilzen	TT	1957	Špídla, V.
Mozart, W. A.	*Cosi Fan Tutte*	Prague	TT	1957	Mandaus, L.
Vishnevski, V.	*Optimistic Tragedy*	Prague	NT	1957	Tovstonogov, G.
Osborne, J.	*Entertainer*	Prague	TT	1957	Radok, A.
Perrini, A.	*Devil's Never Asleep*	Prague	ABCT	1957	Horníček, M.
Dvořák, A.	*Rusalka*	Venice	TLF	1958	Kašlík, V.
Ostrčil, O.	*Jack's Kingdom*	Prague	NT	1958	Thein, H.
Kesselring, J.	*Arsenic and Old Lace*	Prague	ABCT	1958	Roháč, J.
Hrubín, F.	*Sunday in August*	Prague	TT	1958	Krejča, O.
Radok, E.	*Polyekran*	Brussels	EX58	1958	Radok, E.
Radok, A.	*Laterna Magika*	Brussels	EX58	1958	Radok, A.
Janáček, L.	*From the House of the Dead*	Prague	NT	1958	Thein, H.
Janáček, L.	*Jenufa*	Novosibirsk	ST	1958	Michajlov, L.
Smetana, B.	*Bartered Bride*	Prague	NT	1958	Kašlík, V.
Voskovec and Werich	*Big Bertha*	Prague	ABCT	1958	Nesvadba, J.
Tyl, J. K.	*Bagpiper from Strakonice*	Prague	NT	1958	Krejča, O.
Bořkovec, B.	*Paleček*	Prague	SMT	1958	Thein, H.
Pauer, J.	*Zuzana Vojířová*	Prague	NT	1959	Kašlík, V.
Smetana, B.	*Bartered Bride*	Prague	SMT	1959	Kašlík,V.
Hanuš, J.	*Othello*	Prague	NT	1959	Němeček, J.
Wagner, R.	*Flying Dutchman*	Prague	SMT	1959	Kašlík, V.
Kainar, J.	*Sage*	Prague	ABCT	1959	Horníček, M.
Hrubín, F.	*Sunday in August*	Ostrava	ST	1959	Krejča, O.
Handel, G. F.	*Acis and Galatea*	Prague	NT	1959	Thein, H.
Heyduk, J.	*Homecoming*	Prague	TT	1959	Radok, A.
Dvořák, A.	*Rusalka*	Leningrad	ST	1959	Linhart, O.
Miller, A.	*Death of a Salesman*	Prague	TT	1959	Pleskot, J.

Svoboda with Sir Laurence Olivier

AUTHOR	TITLE	CITY	THEATRE	DATE	DIRECTOR
Radok, A.	*Laterna Magika II Program*	Prague	NT	1959	Radok, A.
Kašlík, V.	*Juan*	Prague	TT	1959	Jílek, V.
Janáček, L.	*Káta Kabanová*	Amsterdam	NT	1959	Thein, H.
Leoncavallo, R.	*Pagliacci*	Ostrava	ST	1959	Thein, H.
Puccini, G.	*Gianni Schicchi*	Ostrava	ST	1959	Thein, H.
Topol, J.	*Their Day*	Prague	TT	1959	Krejča, O.
Shakespeare, W.	*Hamlet*	Prague	NT	1959	Pleskot, J.
Janáček, L.	*Travels of Mr. Brouček*	Prague	SMT	1959	Kašlík, V.
Dürrenmatt, F.	*Visit* (not performed)			1959	Radok, A.
Dvořák, A.	*Rusalka*	Prague	NT	1960	Kašlík, V.
Chekhov, A.	*Sea Gull*	Prague	TT	1960	Krejča, O.
Suchoň, E.	*Svatopluk*	Prague	NT	1960	Thein, H.
Illin, E.	*After the Wedding*	Prague	TT	1960	Macháček, M.
Tyl, J. K.	*Drahomíra*	Prague	NT	1960	Krejča, O.
Janáček, L.	*Jenufa*	Amsterdam	NT	1960	Thein, H.
Puccini, G.	*Tosca*	Prague	SMT	1960	Jernek, K.
Dietl, J	*Once There Were Two*	Prague	ABCT	1960	Roháč, J.
Scerbacev, V. V.	*Tobacco Captain*	Prague	KlT	1960	Thein, H.
Novák, V.	*Lantern*	Prague	SMT	1960	Thein, H.
Smetana, B.	*Dalibor*	Prague	NT	1961	Kašlík, V.
Mozart, W. A.	*Marriage of Figaro*	Prague	NT	1961	Jernek, K.
Smetana, B.	*Bartered Bride*	Zagreb	CNT	1961	Roje, N.
Goldoni, G.	*Outburst at Chiozza*	Prague	TT	1961	Macháček, M.
Prokofiev, S.	*Story of a Real Man*	Prague	NT	1961	Ansimov, G.
Hrubín, F.	*Starry Night*	Prague	TT	1961	Krejča, O.
Shaw, G. B.	*Saint Joan*	Pilzen	TT	1961	Špídla, V.
Kalaš, J.	*Indomitability*	Prague	SMT	1961	Thein, H.
Knittel, Z.	*French at the Nizza*	Prague	TA	1961	Thein, H.
Nono, L.	*Intoleranza 1960*	Venice	TLF	1961	Kašlík, V.
Patrick, J.	*Curious Savage*	Prague	ABCT	1961	Hrušinský, R.
Suchoň, E.	*Whirlpool*	Moscow	SOT	1961	Michajlov, L.
Opitz, K.	*My General*	Prague	EFBT	1961	Roháč, J.
Mozart, W. A.	*Magic Flute*	Prague	TT	1961	Kašlík, V.
Karváš, P.	*Antigone and the Others*	Prague	NT	1962	Macháček, M.
Baierl, H.	*Brave Mother Flinca*	Prague	TCA	1962	Dudek, J.
Sebalin, V.	*Taming of the Shrew*	Prague	SMT	1962	Ansimov, G.
Kundera, M.	*Owners of the Keys*	Prague	TT	1962	Krejča, O.
Rossini, G.	*Barber of Seville*	Pilzen	TT	1962	Thein, H.
Doubrava, J.	*Ballad of Love*	Prague	SMT	1962	Štros, L.
Leonov, L.	*Apple Orchard*	Prague	TT	1962	Lohniský, V.
Smetana, B.	*Secret*	Prague	NT	1962	Thein, H.
Fischer, J.	*Romeo, Juliet, Darkness*	Brno	ST	1962	Vězník, V.
Fischer, J.	*Romeo, Juliet, Darkness*	Prague	NT	1962	Thein, H.
Mozart, W. A.	*Don Giovanni*	Prague	TT	1962	Kašlík, V.
Humbálek, G. C.	*No More Heroes in Thebes*	Prague	TB	1962	Krejča, O.
Fibich, Z.	*Tempest*	Olomouc	ST	1962	Thein, H.
Krejčí, I.	*Uproar in Ephesus*	Prague	SMT	1962	Mandaus, L.
Sophocles	*Oedipus Rex*	Prague	SMT	1963	Macháček, M.
Shakespeare, W.	*Twelfth Night*	Prague	TT	1963	Pleskot, J.
Schulhoff, E.	*Sonnambula*	Prague	SMT	1963	Němeček, J.
Prokofiev, S.	*The Prodigal Son*	Prague	SMT	1963	Němeček, J.
Gershwin, G.	*Rhapsody in Blue*	Prague	SMT	1963	Němeček, J.
Opitz, K.	*My General*	W. Berlin	VB	1963	Roháč, J.
Martinů, B.	*Julietta*	Prague	NT	1963	Kašlík, V.
Topol, J.	*Carnival's End*	Olomouc	ST	1963	Krejča, O.
Miller, A	*Death of a Salesman*	Russe, Bulg.	NT	1963	Popov, T.
Dürrenmatt, F.	*Physicists*	Prague	MCT	1963	Vymetal, L.
Prokofiev, S.	*Love for Three Oranges*	Prague	SMT	1963	Ansimov, G.
Shakespeare, W.	*Midsummer Night's Dream*	Prague	NT	1963	Špídla, V.
Dvořák, A.	*Rusalka*	Amsterdam	OH	1963	Kašlík, V.
Rossini, G.	*Italiana in Algeri*	Rio de Janeiro	MT	1963	Ratoo, G.
Shakespeare, W.	*Romeo and Juliet*	Prague	NT	1963	Krejča, O.
Havel, V.	*The Garden Party*	Prague	TB	1963	Krejča, O.
Skála, et. al.	*Dragon's a Dragon*	Prague	RkT	1963	Pleskot, J.
Dvořák, A.	*Dimitrij*	Prague	NT	1963	Thein, H.
Berg, A.	*Wozzek* (not performed)	Rio de Janeiro	MT	1963	Ruberti, S.
Weinberger, J.	*Svanda the Bagpiper* (not performed)	Vienna	VO	1963	Mandaus, L.

AUTHOR	TITLE	CITY	THEATRE	DATE	DIRECTOR
Slomozynski, M.	*Loneliness*	Prague	TT	1964	Macháček, M.
Hindemith, P.	*Cardillac*	Milan	LS	1964	Kašlík, V.
Verdi, G.	*Don Carlos*	Warsaw	GO	1964	Štros, L.
Shakespeare, W.	*Romeo and Juliet*	Havana	TM	1964	Krejča, O.
Shakespeare, W.	*King Lear*	Budapest	NS	1964	Marton, E.
Kašlík, V.	*Don Juan*	Amsterdam	HNB	1964	Jílek, V.
Bellini, V.	*Sonnambula*	Amsterdam	HNB	1964	Balanchine, G.
Stravinsky, I.	*Firebird*	Wiesbaden	ST	1964	Keres and Gora
Janáček, L.	*Káta Kabanová*	Prague	NT	1964	Thein, H.
Rossini, G.	*Barber of Seville*	Prague	SMT	1964	Thein, H.
Smetana, B.	*Dalibor*	Edinburgh	KT	1964	Kašlík, V.
Rozov, V.	*On The Way*	E. Berlin	DT	1964	Meves, H.
Suchoň, E.	*Whirlpool*	Prague	NT	1964	Kašlík, V.
Topol, J.	*Carnival's End*	Prague	TT	1964	Krejča, O.
Dvořák, A.	*Rusalka*	Vienna	VO	1964	Kašlík, V.
Shakespeare, W.	*Hamlet*	Brussels	NT	1965	Krejča, O.
Čapek, K. and J.	*Insect Comedy*	Prague	NT	1965	Macháček, M.
Nono, L.	*Intoleranza*	Boston	OGB	1965	Caldwell, S.
Offenbach, J.	*Orpheus in the Underworld*	Moscow	OT	1965	Ansimov, G.
Verdi, G.	*Otello*	Prague	NT	1965	Thein, H.
Manzoni, G.	*Atomic Death*	Milan	PS	1965	Puecher, V.
Hanuš, J.	*Prometheus' Torch*	Prague	NT	1965	Thein, H.
Turgenev, I.	*Month in the Country*	Prague	TT	1965	Hrušinský, R.
Mahler, Z.	*Mill*	Bratislava	SNT	1965	Krejča, O.
Suchý, J.	*Well Paid Stroll*	Prague	SfT	1965	Roháč, J.
Bizet, G.	*Carmen*	Bremen	GT	1965	Friedrich, G.
Janáček, L.	*Makropulos Affair*	Prague	NT	1965	Kašlík, V.
Miller, A.	*After the Fall*	Prague	TT	1965	Véjrážka, V.
Topol, J.	*Cat on the Rails*	Prague	TBG	1965	Krejča, O.
Tchaikovsky, P. I.	*Queen of Spades* (not performed)	Wiesbaden	ST	1965	Kašlík, V.
Sophocles	*Elektra* (not performed)	Rome		1965	
Chekhov, A.	*Sea Gull*	Brussels	NT	1966	Krejča, O.
Mozart, W. A.	*Don Giovanni*	Bremen	GpT	1966	Friedrich, G.
Hochhuth, R.	*Deputy*	E. Berlin	DT	1966	Meves, H.
Offenbach, J.	*Tales of Hoffmann*	Weisbaden	ST	1966	Kašlík, V.
Testi, F.	*Lower Depths*	Milan	PS	1966	Kašlík, V.
Gorky, M.	*Last Ones*	Prague	TT	1966	Radok, A.
Chekhov, A.	*Three Sisters*	Prague	TBG	1966	Krejča, O.
Shakespeare, W.	*Macbeth*	Milan	TSB	1966	Buazzelli, R.
Ostrovsky, A.	*Storm*	London	NT	1966	Dexter, J.
Wilder, T.	*Skin of our Teeth*	Prague	TT	1966	Pleskot, J.
Smetana, B.	*Bartered Bride*	Dortmund	MT	1966	Vokálek, E.
Smetana, B.	*Bartered Bride*	Mannheim	ST	1966	Kašlík, V.
Giraudoux, J.	*Madwoman of Chaillot*	Prague	TT	1966	Hrušinský, R.
Martinů, B.	*Mary Plays*	Wiesbaden	ST	1966	Kašlík, V
Verdi, G.	*Trovatore*	Berlin	KO	1966	Friedrich, G.
Gounod, C.	*Faust*	Warsaw	TW	1966	Štros, L.
Büchner, G.	*Danton's Death* (not performed)	London	NT	1966	Olivier, L.
Garcia-Lorca, F.	*House of Bernarda Alba*	Prague	TT	1967	Radok, A.
Novotný, Dr.	*Metamorphoses*	Montreal	EX67	1967	Svoboda, J.
Radok, E.	*Diapolyekran-Creation of the World*	Montreal	EX67	1967	Radok, E.
Svoboda, J.	*Polyvision*	Montreal	EX67	1967	Svoboda, J.
Svoboda, J.	*Symphonie*	Montreal	EX67	1967	Svoboda, J.
Strauss, R.	*Frau Ohne Schatten*	London	ROH	1967	Hartmann, R.
Chekhov, A.	*Three Sisters*	London	NT	1967	Olivier, L.
Nestroy, J.	*One-Ended Rope*	Prague	TBG	1967	Krejča, O.
Wagner, R.	*Tristan and Isolde*	Wiesbaden	ST	1967	Drese, C.
Komensky, J. A.	*Labyrinth of the World* (not performed)	Prague	NT	1967	Pleskot, J.
Graves, R.	*Iliad* (not performed)	New York	LC	1967	Wanamaker, S.
Gombrowicz, W.	*Wedding*	W. Berlin	ScT	1968	Schröder, E.
Gounod, C.	*Faust*	Wiesbaden	ST	1968	Kašlík, V.
Dürrenmatt, F.	*Anabaptists*	Prague	NT	1968	Macháček, M.
Sophocles	*Antigone*	Helsinki	NT	1968	Kirimaa, A.
Topol, J.	*Carnival's End*	Vienna	AT	1968	Krejča, O.
Meyerbeer, G.	*Robert Le Diable*	Florence	TC	1968	Wallmann, M.
Brecht, B.	*Threepenny Opera*	Munich	ChT	1968	Grossman, J.

Svoboda with artistic director Wolfgang Wagner

AUTHOR	TITLE	CITY	THEATRE	DATE	DIRECTOR
Weber, C. M. von	*Oberon*	Munich	SO	1968	Hartmann, R.
Tyl, J. K.	*Bagpiper from Strakonice*	Prague	NT	1968	Pleskot, J.
Orff, K.	*Prometheus*	Munich	SO	1968	Everding, A.
Macourek, M.	*Suzanna Play*	Frankfurt/Main	MT	1968	Pleskot, J.
Schnitzler, A.	*Green Cockatoo*	Prague	TBG	1968	Krejča, O.
Topol J.	*Hour of Love*	Prague	TBG	1968	Krejča, O.
Strauss, R.	*Salome* (not performed)	Chicago	COH	1968	Puecher, V.
Offenbach, J.	*Tales of Hoffmann*	W. Berlin	DO	1969	Kašlík, V.
Mozart, W. A.	*Don Giovanni*	Prague	TT	1969	Kašlík, V.
Verdi, G.	*Macbeth*	Cologne	MT	1969	Neugebauer, H.
Werle L. J.	*Journey*	Hamburg	SO	1969	Runsten, L.
Zimmermann, B. A.	*Soldiers*	Munich	SO	1969	Kašlík, V.
Verdi, G.	*Sicilian Vespers*	Hamburg	SO	1969	Dexter, J.
Prokofiev, S.	*Fiery Angel*	Frankfurt/Main	MT	1969	Kašlík, V.
Shakespeare, W.	*Romeo and Juliet*	Cologne	MT	1969	Krejča, O.
Janáček, L.	*Jenufa*	Prague	NT	1969	Thein, H.
Shakespeare, W.	*Macbeth*	Prague	TT	1969	Pleskot, J.
Wagner, R.	*Flying Dutchman*	Bayreuth	FT	1969	Everding, A.
Chekhov, A.	*Sea Gull*	Stockholm	MT	1969	Krejča, O.
Musset, A. de	*Lorenzaccio*	Prague	TBG	1969	Krejča, O.
Garcia-Lorca, F.	*House of Bernarda Alba*	Brussels	TRo	1969	Radok, A.
Debussy, C.	*Pelléas and Melisande*	London	ROH	1969	Kašlík, V.
Wagner, R.	*Tannhäuser*	Hamburg	SO	1969	Mayen, H.
Shakespeare, W.	*Antony and Cleopatra* (not performed)	W.Berlin	ST	1969	Körtner, F.
Zeyer, J. and Suk, J.	*Radůz and Mahulena*	Prague	NT	1970	Zachar, K.
Szokoay, S.	*Hamlet*	Cologne	MT	1970	Neugebauer, H.
Werle, L. J.	*Journey*	Stockholm	RO	1970	Runsten, L.
Boll, H.	*Clown*	Dusseldorf	MT	1970	Radok, A.

Author	Title	City	Theatre	Date	Director
Chekhov, A.	*Ivanov*	Prague	TBG	1970	Krejča, O.
Fry, C.	*Lady's Not for Burning*	Prague	TT	1970	Macháček, M.
Gombrowicz, W.	*Yvone*	W. Berlin	ST	1970	Schröder, E.
Dvořák, A.	*Rusalka*	Munich	TaG	1970	Kašlík, V.
Verdi, G.	*Aida*	Cologne	MT	1970	Blum, W.
Karel, R.	*Death, the Godmother*	Prague	NT	1970	Kašlík, V.
Chekhov, A.	*Three Sisters*	Brussels	NT	1970	Krejča, O.
Offenbach, J.	*Tales of Hoffman*	Frankfurt/Main	MT	1970	Kašlík, V.
Strauss, R.	*Ariadne auf Naxos*	W. Berlin	DO	1970	Selner, G. R.
Shakespeare, W.	*As You Like It*	Prague	TT	1970	Pleskot, J.
Mozart, W. A.	*Magic Flute*	Munich	SO	1970	Rennert, G.
Dostoyevsky, F.	*Idiot*	London	NT	1970	Quayle, A.
Beckett, S.	*Waiting for Godot*	Salzburg	ST	1970	Krejča, O.
Nestroy, J.	*One-Ended Rope*	Dusseldorf	MT	1970	Krejča, O.
Brecht, B.	*Mother Courage*	Prague	TT	1970	Kačer, J.
Verdi, G.	*Don Carlos*	Frankfurt/Main	MT	1970	Kašlík, V
Prokofiev, S.	*Fiery Angel* (not performed)	Milan	LS	1970	Puecher, V.
Shakespeare, W.	*Henry V*	Prague	TT	1971	Macháček, M.
Sophocles	*Oedipus plays & Antigone*	Prague	TBG	1971	Krejča, O.
Mozart, W. A.	*Idomeneo*	Vienna	SO	1971	Kašlík, V.
Wagner, R.	*Meistersinger* (not performed)	Prague	NT	1971	Thein, H.
Büchner, G.	*Wozzek*	Turin	TStb	1971	Peucher, V.
Berg, A.	*Wozzek*	Milan	LS	1971	Puecher, V.
Svoboda, J.	*Noricama*	Nuremberg	NC	1971	Rychman, L.
Dessau, P.	*Lancelot*	Munich	SO	1971	Kašlík, V.

Svoboda with professor Gabor, the creator of holographie

Photo: Helmut J. Wolf

Svoboda with author and director Evald Schorm

Author	Title	City	Theatre	Date	Director
Wagner, R.	*Meistersinger* (not performed)	Nuremberg	MT	1971	Everding, A.
Prokofiev, S.	*Romeo and Juliet*	Prague	NT	1971	Weigl, P.
Tchaikovsky, P. I.	*Eugen Onegin*	Frankfurt/Main	MT	1971	Kašlík, V.
Verdi, G.	*Simone Boccanegra*	Prague	NT	1971	Kašlík, V.
Gombrowicz, W.	*Operetta*	Berlin	ST	1972	Schröder, E.
Janáček, L.	*From the House of the Dead*	Hamburg	SO	1972	Dexter, J.
Chekhov, A.	*Sea Gull*	Prague	TBG	1972	Krejča, O.
Sheridan, R. B.	*School for Scandal*	Prague	NT	1972	Macháček, M.
Verdi, G.	*Nabucco*	London	CG	1972	Kašlík, V.
Strauss, R.	*Don Juan*	Prague	NT	1972	Němeček, J.
Strauss, R.	*Til Eulenspiegel*	Prague	NT	1972	Jílek, V.
Stravinsky, I.	*Rite of Spring*	Prague	NT	1972	Gabzdyl, E.
Stravinsky, I.	*Rake's Progress*	Prague	NT	1972	Jernek, K.
Bizet, G.	*Carmen*	New York	MO	1972	Gentele, G.
Mussorgsky, M. P.	*Boris Godunov*	Hamburg	SO	1972	Dexter, J.
Zindel, P.	*Effect of Gamma Rays*	Prague	NT	1972	Pleskot, J.
Scriabin, A. N.	*Poem of Fire*	Milan	LS	1972	Peucher, V.
Stravinsky, I.	*Firebird*	Copenhagen	RT	1972	Holm, E.
Brecht, B.	*Threepenny Opera*	Zurich	MT	1972	Buckwitz, H.
Suchoň, E.	*Whirlpool*	Prague	NT	1973	Kočí, P.
Janáček, L.	*Káta Kabanová*	Zurich	OH	1973	Buckwitz, H.
Smetana, B.	*Secret*	Prague	NT	1973	Kočí, P.
Stoppard, T.	*Jumpers*	Vienna	BT	1973	Wood, P.
Gorky, M.	*Children of the Sun*	Prague	NT	1973	Kačer, J.
Wagner, R.	*Tannhäuser*	London	CG	1973	Kašlík, V.
Dvorecky, I.	*Man from Elsewhere*	Prague	NT	1973	Macháček, M.
Tchaikovsky, P. I.	*Sleeping Beauty*	Prague	NT	1973	Weigel, P.
Vallejo, A. B.	*Dream of Reason*	Moscow	MAT	1973	Jefremov, O. N.
Verdi, G.	*Sicilian Vespers*	New York	MO	1974	Dexter, J.
Stoppard, T.	*Jumpers*	Washington, D.C.	KC	1974	Wood, P.
Racine, J.	*Phedre*	Ljubljana	SeNT	1974	Pilikian, H. I.
Cikker, J.	*Coriolanus*	Prague	NT	1974	Kočí, P.

Svoboda with Andre Malraux

Author	Title	City	Theatre	Date	Director
Verdi, G.	*Don Carlos*	Cologne	MT	1974	Neugebauer, H.
LM collective	*Prague Carnival*	Prague	LM	1974	Kašlík, V.
Bukovcan, I.	*Snow on the Limba*	Prague	NT	1974	Hudeček, V.
Smetana, B.	*Devil's Wall*	Prague	NT	1974	Kašlík, V.
Wagner, R.	*Tristan and Isolde*	Beyreuth	FT	1974	Everding, A.
Rostand, E.	*Cyrano de Bergerac*	Prague	NT	1974	Macháček, M.
Berlioz, H.	*Trojans*	Geneva	GT	1974	Riber, J. C.
Wagner, R.	*Rheingold*	London	CG	1974	Friedrich, G.
Wagner, R.	*Walküre*	London	CG	1974	Friedrich, G.
Vishnevsky, V.	*Optimistic Tragedy*	Prague	NT	1975	Macháček, M.
Wagner, R.	*Rheingold*	Geneva	GT	1975	Riber, J. C.
Radickov, J.	*Snow Laughed as It Fell*	Prague	NTs	1975	Vymetal, L.
Berlioz, H.	*Symphonie Fantastique*	Paris	NO	1975	Petit, R.
Schiller, F.	*Kabale und Liebe*	Vienna	AT	1975	Klingenberg, G.
Tolstoi, L.	*War and Peace*	Prague	NT	1975	Ansimov, P.
LM collective	*Love in Carnival Colors*	Prague	LM	1975	Kašlík, V.
Weigel, P.	*Bartolucci*	Paris	TPC	1975	Weigel, P.
Beethoven, L.	*Fidelio*	Zurich	OH	1975	Drese, C. H.
Janáček, L.	*Jenufa*	Prague	NT	1975	Kočí, P.
Wagner, R.	*Siegfried*	London	CG	1975	Friedrich, G.
Folta, P.	*Lost Fairy Tale*	Prague	LM	1975	Jireš, J.
Brecht, B.	*Mohagonny*	Geneva	GT	1975	Riber, J. C.
Verdi, G.	*Simone Boccanegra*	Zurich	OH	1975	Kašlík, V.
Grillparzer, F.	*King Otakar*	Vienna	BT	1976	Klingenberg, G.
Wagner, R.	*Walküre*	Geneva	GT	1976	Riber, J. C.
Bizet, G.	*Passion*	Prague	NT	1976	Weigel, P.
Puccini, G.	*Turandot*	Turin	TRg	1976	Riber, J. C.
Beethoven, L.	*Fidelio*	Prague	NT	1976	Kočí, P.
Wagner, R.	*Siegfried*	Geneva	GT	1976	Riber, J. C.
Verdi, G.	*Otello*	Paris	NO	1976	Hands, T.
Tchaikovsky, P. I.	*Queen of Spades*	Ottawa	NAC	1976	Kašlík, V.
Wagner, R.	*Götterdämmerung*	London	CG	1976	Friedrich, G.
Shakespeare, W.	*Tempest*	Munich	BeT	1976	Schröder, E.
Vrchlický, J.	*Trial of Love*	Prague	NT	1976	Pleskot, J.
Zimmermann, B. A.	*Soldaten*	Hamburg	SO	1976	Friedrich, G.
Verdi, G.	*Don Carlos*	Geneva	GT	1977	Riber, J. C.
Schorm, E., Srnec	*Magic Circus*	Prague	LM	1977	Schorm, E.

AUTHOR	TITLE	CITY	THEATRE	DATE	DIRECTOR
Stieber, M.	*Last Vacation*	Prague	NT	1977	Macháček, M.
Gounod, C.	*Faust*	Berlin	SO	1977	Kašlík, V.
Wagner, R.	*Götterdämmerung*	Geneva	GT	1977	Riber, J. C.
Strauss, R.	*Ariadne auf Naxos*	Ottawa	NAC	1977	Kašlík, V.
Dürrenmatt, F.	*Angel Comes to Babylon*	Zurich	OH	1977	Friedrich, G.
Gelman, A.	*Feedback*	Moscow	MAT	1977	Jefremov, O. N.
Vasiljev, B.	*White Storks above Brest*	Prague	MT	1977	Hudeček, V.
Strauss, R.	*Frau ohne Schatten*	Geneva	GT	1978	Riber, J. C.
Verdi, G.	*Macbeth*	Prague	NT	1978	Kašlík, V.
Verdi, G.	*Trovatore*	Zurich	OH	1978	Enriquez, F.
Goldoni, C.	*Campiello*	Prague	NT	1978	Macháček, M.
Janáček, L.	*Jenufa*	New York	JS	1978	Freedman, G.
Verdi, G.	*Nabucco*	Geneva	GT	1978	Klingenberg, G.
Wagner, R.	*Tristan and Isolde*	Geneva	GT	1978	Riber, J. C.
Smetana, B.	*Bartered Bride*	New York	MO	1978	Dexter, J.
Wagner, R.	*Meistersinger*	Prague	NT	1978	Kašlík, V.
Janáček, L.	*From the House of the Dead*	Zurich	OH	1978	Friedrich, G.
Beethoven, L.	*Fidelio*	Geneva	GT	1978	Drese, C. H.
Verdi, G.	*Traviata*	Prague	NT	1979	Weigel, P.
Janáček, L.	*Makropulos Affair*	Hannover	ST	1979	Kašlík, V.
Stroupežnický, L.	*Our Militants*	Prague	NT	1979	Macháček, M.
Andersen, H. C.	*Snow Queen*	Prague	LM	1979	Schorm, E.
Hašek J.	*Good Soldier Schweik*	Berlin	ScT	1979	Buckwitz, H.
Puccini, G.	*Sister Angelique, Gianni Schicchi*	Banff	NAC	1979	Major, L.
Petit, R.	*Parisiana*	Marseilles	MT	1979	Petit, R.
Verdi, G.	*Don Carlos*	Zurich	OH	1979	Riber, J. C.
Čapek, K.	*White Disease*	Prague	TT	1980	Macháček, M.
Strindberg	*Dream Play*	Albany, N. Y.	SUNY	1980	Burian, J.
Bartok, B.	*Miraculous Mandarin*	Milan	LS	1980	Petit, R.
Janáček, L.	*Jenufa*	Geneva	GT	1980	Schorm, E.
Dvořák, A.	*Rusalka*	Stuttgart	ST	1980	Schorm, E.
Fišer, L.	*Grief over the Message from Ur*	Prague	NT	1980	Kura, M.
Zeljenka, I.	*Hero*	Prague	NT	1980	Pokorný, F.
Kučera, V.	*Flawless Life*	Prague	NT	1980	Blázek, J.
Verdi, G.	*Otello*	Geneva	GT	1980	Riber, J. C.
McDonald, B.	*Time out of Mind*	Banff	NAC	1980	McDonald, B.
Dáněk, O.	*Dutchess of Wallenstein's A*	Prague	NT	1980	Macháček, M.
Máša, A.	*Night Rehearsal*	Prague	LM	1981	Schorm, E.
Strauss, R.	*Josef's Legende*	Milan	LS	1981	Flindt, F.
Goethe, J. W.	*Faust*	Prague	NT	1981	Hudeček, V.
Mozart, W. A.	*Idomeneo*	Ottawa	NAC	1981	Kašlík, V.
Orff, K.	*Die Kluge*	Prague	SMT	1981	Jernek, K.
Bartok, B.	*Duke Bluebeard's Castle*	Prague	SMT	1981	Jernek, K.
Janáček, L.	*From the House of the Dead*	Berlin	DO	1981	Friedrich, G.
Offenbach, J.	*Tales of Hoffmann*	Prague	SMT	1981	Darrell, P.
Aeschylus	*Oresteia*	Prague	TT	1981	Schorm, E.
Strauss, R.	*Elektra* (Euro TV)	Munich		1981	Friedrich, G.
Kašlík, V.	*Road*	Prague	SMT	1982	Jernek, K.
Tchaikovsky, P. I.	*Queen of Spades*	Houston	HO	1982	Kašlík, V.
Shakespeare, W.	*Hamlet*	Prague	NT	1982	Macháček, M.
Smetana, B.	*Dalibor*	Prague	SMT	1982	Kašlík, V.
Kašlík, V.	*The Road*	Prague	SMT	1982	Jernek, K.
Tchaikovsky P. I.	*Queen of Spades*	Houston	HO	1982	Kašlík, V.
Tchaikovsky P. I.	*Swan Lake*	Milan	LS	1982	Beriozoff, N.
Shakespeare, W.	*Hamlet*	Prague	NT	1982	Macháček, M.
Smetana, B.	*Dalibor*	Prague	SMT	1982	Kašlík, V.
Pogodin, N.	*Aristocrats*	Prague	NT	1982	Hudeček, V.
Claudel, P.	*Exchange*	Paris	Od	1982	Delcampe, A.
Handel, G. F.	*Saul*	Zurich	OH	1982	Drese, C. H.
Zeyer, J.	*Old Story*	Prague	NT	1983	Pleskot, J.
Orff, K.	*Antigone*	Zurich	OH	1983	Everding, A.
Pauer, J.	*Talkative Snail*	Prague	LM	1983	Pojar, B.
Smetena, B.	*Libuše*	Praha	NT	1983	Jernek, K.
Tyl, J. K.	*Bagpiper of Strakonice*	Praha	NT	1983	Hudeček, V.
Gogol, N. V.	*Dead Souls*	Aulnay	TL	1983	Ulusoy, M.
Honegger, A.	*Saint Joan*	Zurich	OH	1983	Drese, C. H.
Verdi, G.	*Macbeth*	Montreal	OH	1983	Kašlík, V.

Author	Title	City	Theatre	Date	Director
collective	*Time out of Mind*	Zurich	OH	1984	Macdonald, B.
Buck, E.	*Theatre, Mirror of the World*	Cologne	MM	1984	Buck, E.
Donizetti, G.	*Mary Stuart*	Zurich	OH	1984	Asagaroff, G.
Pirandello, L.	*Six Characters*	Louvain	TS	1984	Delcampe, A.
Verdi, G.	*Sicillian Vespers*	London	NO	1984	Dexter, J.
Claudel, P.	*Break of Noon*	Louvain	TS	1984	Delcampe, A.
Verdi, G.	*Sicillian Vespers*	Amsterdam	OH	1984	Dexter, J.
Tyl, J. K.	*Miners of Kutná Hora*	Prague	NT	1984	Hudeček, V.
Mozart, W. A.	*Don Giovanni*	Prague	NT	1984	Kašlík, V.
Strauss, R.	*Salome*	Montreal	OH	1985	Kašlík, V.
Verdi, G.	*Macbeth*	Zurich	OH	1985	Asagaroff, G.
Constant, M.	*Blue Angel*	Berlin	OH	1985	Petit, R.
Chekhov, A.	*Cherry Orchard*	Sofia	NT	1985	Chalacev
Pettit, R.	*Puss in Boots*	Paris	PC	1985	Petit, R.
Verdi, G.	*Nabucco*	Zurich	OH	1986	Dexter, J.
Wagner, R.	*Flying Dutchman*	Prague	NT	1986	Kašlík, V.
Puccini, G.	*Turandot*	Turin	TRg	1986	Asagaroff, R. G.
Sobol, J.	*Ghetto*	Oslo	NT	1986	Sem, I. Mrs.
Macdonald, B.	*Steps*	Vancouver	QET	1986	Macdonald, B.
Mann, T.	*Death in Venice* (Ballet)	Munich	OH	1986	Věsák, N.
Kašlík, V.	*Rogue's Ballad*	Prague	NT	1986	Kašlík, V.
Kopit, A.	*End of the World*	Prague	NT	1986	Laurin, F.
Janáček, L.	*Jenufa*	Marseille	OH	1986	Schorm, E.
Petit, R.	*Anna Pavlova*	Barcelona		1986	Petit, R.
Ibsen, H.	*Little Eyolf*	Washington	ET	1986	Dexter, J.
Janáček, L.	*Káta Kabanová*	Prague	NT	1986	Jernek, K.
Schorm, E. et. al.	*Odysseus*	Prague	LM	1987	Schorm, E. et. al.
Shakespeare, W.	*Twelfth Night*	Schonbrun	ST	1987	Windisch-Spoerk, N.
Verdi, G.	*Don Carlos*	Bonn	MT	1987	Riber, J. C.
Stravinski, I.	*Oedipus Rex*	Prague	NT	1987	Schorm, E.
Martinů, B.	*Ariadne*	Prague	NT	1987	Schorm, E.
Gorky, M.	*Jegor Bulycov*	Prague	NT	1987	Laurin, F.
May, I. G.	*Alesio*	Madrid	NT	1987	Planella, P.
Brecht, B.	*He Who Says Yes...No*	Milan	PT	1988	Puggelli, L.
Chekhov, A.	*Seagull*	Louvain	TS	1988	Delcampe, A.
Delaney, S.	*Taste of Honey*	Prague	NT	1988	Macháček, M.
Dürrenmatt, F.	*Achterloo IV*	Schwetzinger	RKT	1988	Dürrenmatt, F.
Wagner, R.	*Rheingold*	Orange	RmT	1988	Riber, J. C.
Wagner, R.	*Walküre*	Orange	RmT	1988	Riber, J. C.
Wagner, R.	*Siegfried*	Orange	RmT	1988	Riber, J. C.
Wagner, R.	*Götterdämmerung*	Orange	RmT	1988	Riber, J. C.
Hampton, C.	*Liasons Dangereuse*	Prague	NT	1988	Smoček, L.
Goethe, J. W.	*Faust I*	Milan	PT	1988	Strehler, G.
Strindberg, A.	*Pelican*	Louvain	TS	1989	Delcampe, A.
Dürrenmatt, F.	*Collaborator*	Aachen	OH	1989	Kehr, S.
Cozotte, J.	*Amorous Devil*	Fiesole	TRF	1989	Petit, R.
Delcampe. A.	*Jacques Brell*	Liege	CR	1989	Delcampe, A.
Muller, H.	*Task*	Haifa	NT	1989	Brockhaus, H.
Dürrenmatt, F.	*Minotaur*	Prague	LM	1989	Svoboda, J.
Verdi, G.	*Force of Destiny*	Vienna	OH	1989	del Monaco, C.
Ibsen, H.	*Ghosts*	Antwerp	RaT	1989	Windisch-Spoerk, N.
Seufer, J.	*Vineta*	Vienna	ST	1990	Windisch-Spoerk, N.
Moliere	*Bourgeois Gentleman*	Louvain	ST	1990	Delcampe, A.
Verdi, G.	*Luisa Miller*	Trieste	TGV	1990	Girardi, F.
Marivaux	*Game of Love and Chance*	Antwerp	RaT	1990	Tillemans, W.
Smetana, B.	*Bartered Bride*	Stuttgart	ST	1990	del Monaco, C.
Brecht, B.	*Seven Deadly Sins*	Dusseldorf	ST	1990	Brockhaus, H.
Strauss, R.	*Salome*	Berlin	OH	1990	Weigel, P.
Krofta	*Premiere* (not performed)	Prague	LM	1990	
Mozart, W. A.	*Don Giovanni*	Trieste	TGV	1990	Girardi, F.
Dvořák, A.	*Rusalka*	Prague	NT	1991	Windisch-Spoerk, N.
Ibsen, H.	*Lady from the Sea*	Milan	PT	1991	Brockhaus, H.
Goethe, J. W.	*Faust II*	Milan	PT	1991	Strehler, G.

Author	Title	City	Theatre	Date	Director
Gogol, N.	*Inspector General*	Albany	SUNY	1991	Burian, J.
Verdi, G.	*Traviata*	Prague	NT	1991	Weigel, P.
Vallejo, A. B.	*Dream of Reason*	Antwerp	MT	1991	Tillemans, V.
Dürrenmatt, F.	*Collaborator*	Hamburg	TG	1991	Scharlotte, K.
Schnitzler, A.	*The Return of Cascnova*	Benevento	PR	1991	Delcampe, A.
Frisch, M.	*Biedermann and the Firebugs*	Antwerp	RaT	1991	Brockhaus, H.
Verdi, G.	*Masked Ball*	Wuppertal	OH	1991	Brockhaus,H.
Shakespeare, W.	*Twelfth Night*	Antwerp	RaT	1991	Tillemans, W.
Mussorgsky, M. P.	*Boris Godunov* (not performed)	Moscow	MAT	1991	Jefremov, O.
Renato, S.	*Ravensbruck*	Antwerp	RaT	1992	Windisch-Spoerk, N.
Shaw, G. B.	*Pygmalion*	Prague	NT	1992	Hrusinsky, R.
Nestroy, J.	*One-Ended Rope*	Prague	BGT	1992	Krejča, O.
Mozart, W. A.	*Magic Flute*	Prague	LM	1992	Helge, L.
Verdi, G.	*La Traviata*	Macerata	OH	1992	Brockhaus, H.
Bellini, V.	*La Sonnambula*	Macerata	OH	1992	Brockhaus, H.
Gogol, N.	*Inspector General*	Antwerp	MT	1992	Smoček, L.
Meir, G. van	*Faleryn*	Antwerp	MT	1992	Tillemans, W.

INDEX

DATE DUE		
Study 8-30-14		
	WITHDRAWN	